70 Reflections

on Trusting God

Comfort and Counsel for Christian

Women Who Love God and Yet Feel

Trapped in a Difficult Situation

Katie Hoffman

As a Special Gift to My Readers

I always offer one or more free books on my website—and you can choose what book you would like by going to www.katiehoffman.org/freebooks.

Some of the available choices may include:

- How to Have a Wonderful Marriage

- The Secret of Joy

- Finding Strength in the Joy of the LORD

- Between Here and Glory

Visit www.katiehoffman.org/freebooks to see the current selection.

To my wonderful husband Todd, my companion in trusting God through many difficult times.

Contents

As a Special Gift to My Readers iii

Introduction 1

Reflections 1-10 ~ The Choice to be Thankful 4

Reflections 11-20 ~ Believing that God is Good 18

Reflections 21-30 ~ Believing that God is Sovereign 38

Reflections 31-40 ~ Trusting God in Difficult Times 71

Reflections 41-50 ~ Becoming the Servant of All 100

Reflections 51-60 ~ Believing God's Grace is Sufficient 120

Reflections 61-70 ~ Victory in Trusting God 142

Epilogue: How to be Content With Your Calling 162

Bonus Content: Earth is Not Enough 172

"Blessed is the man who trusts in the LORD

And whose trust is the LORD.

For he will be like a tree planted by the water,

That extends its roots by a stream

And will not fear when the heat comes;

But its leaves will be green,

And it will not be anxious in a year of drought

Nor cease to yield fruit."

Jeremiah 17:7-8

Introduction

For many of us in the midst of trials, we might seem happy and content on the outside, but inside we are fighting a war. Depending on the trial or why it's happening, we may spend our time thinking about things we wish we had, regretting decisions we've made, or replaying what we wished we would have said or done in past situations.

I've been there. Like Shadrach, Meshach, and Abednego, I've found myself at the bottom of a furnace with the heat turned up seven times. But God was with me in the blazing fire, showing His faithfulness and reminding me that He is sovereign over every flame. He helped me to remember that He is wise and powerful and working everything in my life together for good. (Romans 8:28) He reminded me that instead of feeling sorry for myself, I needed to trust Him and even praise Him.

Somehow there is a blessing to be found in trials. It was during one of those times in the furnace that these seventy reflections were written. When I understand that God has appointed my days in advance according to His perfect purposes and incomprehensible love, then I can thank Him and trust Him even when I don't understand what He is doing. (Psalm 139:16)

I'm excited for you to read these seventy reflections on trusting God. Some are longer and some are a bit shorter, but I pray you will be encouraged by the same truths that also gave me hope. Each reflection begins with one or more Bible verses. Sometimes a part of a verse may be underlined for emphasis and those underlines are mine.

I feel so thankful to say that a few months after I wrote the rough draft of this book, God lifted me out of the furnace. I am amazed by all God has done.

Seeing God's purpose in my suffering, and knowing the work He did in my heart, I am sad that I ever mistrusted God's goodness, that I became like the Israelites who "forgot His deeds and His miracles that He had shown them" (Psalm 78:11). They didn't believe God because they couldn't remember all He had done for them.

Introduction

We serve a God who loves us immeasurably, but suffering can cloud our vision of His love. We may cling to Christ and yet wonder why things aren't changing. We may trust that He is sovereign and yet still think of who we can blame for our situation.

But the truth is, as a believer, you are God's masterpiece and He is making you into the likeness of Christ. There is a great mystery at work in your life, and that is Christ in you, the hope of glory. God has appointed for you an inheritance that is beyond comprehension as a joint-heir with Christ. But you have not received that inheritance yet, and life on earth is painful and hard. I hope this book will remind you of God's goodness, love, and wisdom—and give you strength to trust Him so that you may find rest for your soul.

God reminded me of His goodness and helped me see His faithfulness. Like the Psalmist says in Psalm 23, He restored my soul. And He can restore your soul also.

Reflections 1–10 ~ The Choice to be Thankful

1. "Now to Him who is able to do far more abundantly beyond all that we ask or think, according to the power that works within us, to Him be the glory in the church and in Christ Jesus to all generations forever and ever. Amen" (Ephesians 3:20-21).

God can do what we could never do. He can work in ways that we could never work. And so He can accomplish things that we could never imagine.

God's is powerfully at work in your life—but the intent of that power is not to keep you from suffering—but to accomplish *in you* more than everything you could ask or think. We can't see the finished product of our lives. But in the midst of whatever is happening, we have a beautiful truth about God: "[He] is able to do far more abundantly beyond all that we ask or think."

God is able to do far more than we have even imagined! But sometimes we might wonder if He is even working at all. Because we can't see what is happening inside of us, we may doubt He is working. But we have a promise that He is doing far more than we have asked, far more than we have prayed!

We don't need to see the work, but only trust that He is working. While we may not see all He is doing, we can thank Him for what we can see.

The point of our thankfulness is not to make us feel great, but to acknowledge that God is great. Having a thankful heart is about making much of the great, glorious God who would so freely and abundantly choose to bless us. Our goal in thankfulness is to offer praise to the only wise God and to focus on Him, knowing He is sufficient for all we need.

"I will give thanks to You, O Lord my God, with all my heart, and will glorify Your name forever. For Your lovingkindness toward me is great, and You have delivered my soul from the depths of Sheol" (Psalm 86:12-13).

For additional reflection: What has God already done for you that you can thank Him for today? How has God "delivered your soul from the depths of Sheol"?

2. "Therefore we do not lose heart, but though our outer man is decaying, yet our inner man is being renewed day by day. For momentary, light affliction is producing for us an eternal weight of glory far beyond all comparison, while we look not at the things which are seen, but at the things which are not seen; for the things which are seen are temporal, but the things which are not seen are eternal" (2 Corinthians 4:16-18).

The problem with unthankfulness is that it exalts our circumstances over God's goodness and sovereignty. We become so focused on our disappointments that we miss God's work in our lives.

The truth is, even though our *seen* circumstances may be bad, our *unseen*, eternal circumstances are beyond good.

Though we may sometimes have painful and difficult circumstances here on earth, things are still *good* for us as believers. My name is written in heaven, right now. I have an inheritance waiting for me, right now. Those are my unseen but still very real circumstances.

Because we know Jesus all the time, because we are redeemed all the time, because God loves us all the time, we can have joy because it is well with our soul. And that is good, good, good news. It's what gives us hope in the midst of our present and sorrowful circumstances.

For additional reflection: When you think of the things that provoke self pity—regrets, unfulfilled desires, a difficult relationship, suffering—what specific things can you do to focus on God's goodness and your eternal inheritance when these thoughts or situations arise?

3. "In everything give thanks; for this is God's will for you in Christ Jesus" (1 Thessalonians 5:18).

When I think about what God wants me to do here on earth, I often forget that one of my primary jobs is to spend my life in thanksgiving. Giving thanks in everything can be one of the hardest things we will do, but we must remember that thankfulness is God's will for our life.

Thankfulness is also what protects us from discontentment. Discontentment keeps the Christian from experiencing the blessed, peaceful, and joyful life God can give. If we want to trust God fully, we must learn to give thanks always, regardless of what is actually happening in our lives.

Because it's so easy to forget to be thankful, we need to make a deliberate, conscious effort every day to praise God and give thanks in everything. Giving thanks for the way things are *right now* brings us one step closer to fully trusting God and His plan for our life.

For additional reflection: Looking at the following verses, how did the Psalmist make sure he would thank and praise God every day?

"Seven times a day I praise You, because of Your righteous ordinances" (Psalm 119:164).

8

"At midnight I shall rise to give thanks to You because of Your righteous ordinances" (Psalm 119:62).

Choose one of thing you are thankful for today and write a sentence to the Lord thanking Him for this.

4. "Be filled with the Spirit...always giving thanks for all things in the name of our Lord Jesus Christ to God, even the Father" (Ephesians 5:18b,20).

There are two times when it is crucial that we give thanks to God. The first is when things are going well and we might be tempted to forget the blessings are entirely from God. The second is when things are not going well and we feel the ache of discouragement or the struggle of temptation or the drudgery of sameness or the sting of pain.

And in these two times we are called to give thanks to God, continually remembering His goodness and faithfulness.

9

If we start to feel sorry for ourselves, to dream of things to be different, or to complain about the circumstances we are in, we have forsaken thankfulness to indulge in discontentment.

Discontentment grieves over the things it doesn't have or has to put up with. Thankfulness rejoices over the things it already has. Thankfulness has eyes to see the blessings in every circumstance.

For additional reflection: What provokes you to feel sorry for yourself? How would you describe discontentment in your own life?

5. "Father, if You are willing, remove this cup from Me; yet not My will, but Yours be done" (Luke 22:42).

The night of Jesus' crucifixion, He knew the torture and pain that awaited Him. And so He prayed, "Father, if You are willing, remove this cup from Me; yet not My will, but Yours be done" (Luke 22:42). He asked God to change the plan, to let things be done another way. But since there was no other way—Jesus had to die for our sins and rise from the dead so we can be reconciled to God—Jesus willingly suffered and died. He humbly prayed to the Father, "Your will be done."

When we accept God's plan for our lives with thankfulness, we can pray also pray to the Father, "Your will be done."

In the book, *The Hiding Place*, Corrie Ten Boom describes her experiences living in concentration camps as punishment for housing Jews. In the concentration camps, Corrie and her sister Betsie secretly kept a Bible with them. They read the Bible nightly and clung to its truth. After being moved into new barracks, Corrie found the place swarming with fleas. Betsie reminded Corrie to "give thanks" though they didn't understand God's purpose in allowing so many fleas to torture them.

In the new housing, twice a night the sisters held a worship service in their dormitory. While guards were always present in the dining room and the other areas, they never entered the dormitory.

Then one day Betsie learned why they enjoyed a level of privacy in the dorm so great they could hold full nightly worship services. The guards never entered the room while they prayed and shared Scripture *because of the fleas.* What they thought was difficult was God's hand protecting them from the guards and greater difficulty.

When we give thanks, we must remember that we might never fully know on this earth what God is doing behind the scene. Our job is not to fully grasp what God is doing but to fully give thanks for what He is doing.

For additional reflection: What would it look like in your life to say to God, "Your will be done" and to accept your current circumstances with thankfulness?

6. "It is God who is at work in you, both to will and to work for His good pleasure. Do all things without grumbling or disputing" (Philippians 2:13-14).

The Choice to be Thankful

"The LORD hears your grumblings which you grumble against Him. And what are we? Your grumblings are not against us but against the LORD" (Exodus 16:8).

When we grumble in our heart about each problem in our life, we are fostering an attitude of bitterness and self-pity. When we choose to trade every disappointment for a prayer of thankfulness and blessing, we become free from the bondage of self-pity.

If you find yourself thinking of the difficulty of your situation and feeling frustration or anger over it, pause to consider what God is doing in your life and tell Him "Thank You."

For additional reflection: What can help you remember to give thanks to God whenever you feel tempted to complain or feel frustration in difficult situations?

Why do you think the Bible says that any complaining is "against the Lord"?

7. "O LORD, You are my God; I will exalt You, I will give thanks to Your name; For You have worked wonders, plans formed long ago, with perfect faithfulness" (Isaiah 25:1).

When a woman is fully trusting God, she does not need to worry about her circumstances. She does not need to feel anxious about God's provision, but her greatest concern is to please God and seek first His kingdom.

In times of difficulty and uncertainty, remember that God works in perfect faithfulness to accomplish His plans. His work is wonderful. All the ruins will be restored, all the tears will be wiped away, all reproach will be removed, and all suffering will be replaced with glory. What we don't know now, we will one day fully know.

And so we give thanks today with the anticipation of what God will one day complete.

For additional reflection: Take a moment to pray that God would help you thank Him today because He works His plans with perfect faithfulness.

8. "Blessed is the man whom You chasten, O LORD, and whom You teach out of Your law" (Psalm 94:12).

It is not the absence of pain or hardship which makes for a blessed life, but the presence of thankfulness and praise in the midst of affliction. Suffering gives us opportunities to trust God in ways that ease and prosperity cannot.

For additional reflection: Do you find it odd that the person God disciplines is called "blessed"?

What reason does the following verse give for our suffering?

"If children, heirs also, heirs of God and fellow heirs with Christ, if indeed we suffer with Him so that we may also be glorified with Him" (Romans 8:17).

9. "Oh give thanks to the LORD, for He is good, for His lovingkindness is everlasting" (Psalm 107:1).

There are many things we may feel we need and not have—healing, a child, financial resources, a godly husband, and so much more—but we don't know what God has planned on the road ahead. And because we don't know what is coming, we don't know what we might need. But God knows the journey ahead, and He has "packed" for us exactly what is required. He has given us what we need for where we are right now, and He will continue to give us what we need for what is to come.

So while we may not know what lies before us, we know Who has planned the way. And because we trust that God is good, and that He lovingly, kindly appoints our lives and even the fires that refine us, we thank Him.

For additional reflection: In what ways have you seen God's goodness toward you in the past? How does reflecting on what God has already given you help you thank Him today?

10. "Through Him then, let us continually offer up a <u>sacrifice of praise</u> to God, that is, the fruit of lips that give thanks to His name" (Hebrews 13:15).

We will have to keep making the choice between thankfulness and trusting God or anger, self-pity, worry, and discontentment. We have to choose to believe that God is good because the Bible says so, even when our circumstances seem to suggest otherwise.

Without a thankful heart, a person can become so focused on what they don't have that the disappointment is agonizing. The more we zoom in on what's not right, what we don't have, or what we might never experience, we lose sight of all the good things we have received or will receive from God.

When we take a step back to look at every blessing we have, every gift we've received, and everything God has done for us, the easier it becomes to offer sincere praise for God's goodness toward us.

For additional reflection: In Hebrews 13:15, praise is called a "sacrifice." Why do you think this might be so?

Reflections 11–20 ~ Believing that God is Good

11. "Are not two sparrows sold for a cent? And yet not one of them will fall to the ground apart from your Father...So do not fear; you are more valuable than many sparrows" (Matthew 10:29, 31).

Not even a sparrow can die without God allowing it to happen, and you are far more precious to God than MANY sparrows.

Nothing will happen to you outside of what God allows. God has preordained your life and every day in it before you were even born: "In Your book were all written the days that were ordained for me, when as yet there was not one of them" (Psalm 139:16).

God prepared every good work you would do before you even breathed your first breath: "For we are His workmanship, created in Christ Jesus for good works, which God prepared beforehand so that we would walk in them" (Ephesians 2:10).

God chose YOU, not just before you were born, not just before you came out of your mother's womb, but before He even created the world! "Just as He chose us in Him before the foundation of the world, that we would be holy and blameless before Him. In love He predestined us to adoption as sons through Jesus Christ to Himself, according to the kind intention of His will" Ephesians 1:4-5).

Think of how much you mean to God. He chose you as His own before He created the world, ordained good works for you to do, and wrote the exact number of days you would live. If He cared about you this much before you were even born, be certain that He cares about you right now. "[Cast] all your anxiety on Him, because He cares for you" (1 Peter 5:7).

I have found that the attentiveness God has toward me is one of the most comforting things I can meditate on when life is hard. When my heart is troubled, when I feel pressured, when I'm broken, or when my feelings have been crushed or hurt—to know God sees and cares about that pain or trouble is greatly comforting.

For additional reflection: What verse in this reflection most impacts you and why?

12. "Every good thing given and every perfect gift is from above, coming down from the Father of lights, with whom there is no variation or shifting shadow" (James 1:17).

God is always holy and right in what He does. He does not sin or make mistakes. In our lives, He does what will be eternally good and best for us. He is the giver of everything we have and know about goodness.

How sweet God is that He would willingly give us good gifts though He is so great and we are so undeserving. But often, we might overlook many of His gifts because we don't realize they are gifts. We don't thank Him for what He gives because we don't realize it was from Him.

Instead of thanking Him, sometimes we call the gifts "obstacles, problems, frustrations."

The secret to constant thankfulness is praising God for even the things that don't seem to be from Him. It is believing that God remains good and His plans for us remain good, whatever we may see at the time. When we give thanks for those things that don't seem "thank-worthy," we are deepen our trust in God.

"You are good and do good; teach me Your statutes" (Psalm 119:68).

For additional reflection: What things in your life seem to be too small or too disappointing to thank God for? Can you thank God now for even those things?

13. "Our fathers in Egypt did not understand Your wonders; they did not remember Your abundant kindnesses, but rebelled by the sea, at the Red Sea. Nevertheless He saved them for the sake of His name,

that He might make His power known...The waters covered their adversaries; not one of them was left. Then they believed His words; they sang His praise. They quickly forgot His works" (Psalm 106:7-8, 12-13a).

Spiritual Alzheimer's can often result in doubting God's goodness. We get this condition when we forget God's past faithfulness to us. The Israelites suffered greatly from Spiritual Alzheimer's.

While slaves in Egypt, the Israelites cried out to God for deliverance. He sent Moses to stand before Pharaoh and ask for them to be set free. Pharaoh agreed to let the people go but then quickly changed his mind. Each time Pharaoh refused to let the Israelites go, God sent plagues on the Egyptians. After ten plagues, Pharaoh finally relented and let the Israelites leave Egypt. (Exodus 5-12)

After the Israelites left, Pharaoh changed his mind again and pursued them with all the chariots of Egypt. The Israelites were trapped with the Red Sea on one side and the Egyptian Army quickly approaching on the other side. Moses cried to the LORD and He parted the waters of the Sea so all the Israelites crossed over on dry land. When Pharaoh and all the Egyptian army followed the Israelites into the Sea, the wheels of their chariots clogged with mud and became stuck. As soon as the Israelites finished crossing, the water returned to normal and all the Egyptian army drowned. (Exodus 14)

The Israelites rejoiced! They knew God saved them. He delivered them from Egypt so they would no longer be slaves. He drowned their enemies so they didn't need to be afraid of being chased. They saw miracle after miracle.

But sadly, their thankfulness didn't last. The Bible tells us the progression. "Then they believed His words; they sang His praise. They quickly forgot His works" (Psalm 106:12-13a).

It didn't matter how much God did for them, how often He saved them. They would forget and then complain. As soon as trouble came, "they forgot His deeds and His miracles that He had shown them" (Psalm 78:11). Because they didn't remember what God had done for them in the past, it kept them from believing God in the present.

Instead of continuing to trust God, "they rebelled against Him in the wilderness and grieved Him in the desert!

Again and again they tempted God, and pained the Holy One of Israel. <u>They did not remember His power</u>, the day when He redeemed them from the adversary" (Psalm 78:40-42).

Their unbelief, their complaining, their frustration with Moses, and their self-pity were all tied to their Spiritual Alzheimer's, their forgetfulness of what God had done for them.

For additional reflection: Have there ever been times in your life when you wondered if God was still faithful, if He was still taking care of you perfectly? Was it easy to remember God's past faithfulness during those times?

14. "Those twelve stones which they had taken from the Jordan, Joshua set up at Gilgal. He said to the sons of Israel, 'When your children ask their fathers in time to come, saying, "What are these stones?" then you shall

inform your children, saying, "Israel crossed this Jordan on dry ground""(Joshua 4:20-24).

After forty years of wandering in the wilderness, it was time for the Israelites to enter the promised land. To get there, God parted the Jordan river. This time, God had Joshua and the Israelites collect stones from the middle of the river and set them up at Gilgal. When the children would later ask, "What are these stones?," their father's would tell them about what God had done. (Joshua 4)

I keep a rock on a candle pedestal in my living room as a reminder of a time when God provided a place for us to live during a difficult financial season.

We need to remember what God does for us. During the emotional high of newly answered prayer, we think we'll never forget. But we are over-confident. It's too easy to forget God's faithfulness. If it wasn't so easy, we would trust God far more and never doubt what He is doing in our lives.

Don't let Spiritual Alzheimer's keep you from seeing God's hand in your life. Set up stones in your life so that when it's hard to see what God is doing, you can remember the things He has already done.

When the Israelites didn't trust God, it wasn't because they were unfamiliar with His willingness and power to deliver them. They had seen Him work! He punished them for their lack of faith because it was a direct result of their forgetfulness.

Most of us have seen God answer prayer. We've seen His faithfulness. But when we don't remember what God has done, we doubt His goodness in our lives. We must purposefully remember how God has saved and helped us so we can recount His faithfulness when we are tempted to doubt.

For additional reflection: What things has God done for you in the past? Write down some of these things so that in the years to come, you don't forget God's faithfulness.

15. "And now, Lord, for what do I wait? My hope is in You" (Psalm 39:7).

This verse impacts me most after times of disappointment, when my plans don't work or a dream is crushed. God will tenderly remind me of this verse and I will pray, "And now, Lord, for what do I wait? My hope is in You. It has always been you Lord. You are my hope and my expectation. I'm sorry for putting my hope in other things and letting them distract me. You are the fountain that will never fail and the hope that will never disappoint."

When we long for a better life, a change in circumstances, a way to escape our current trial, and that longing keeps us preoccupied so that our hope is no longer in the Lord, we've forgotten that life is about Jesus. When we yearn for a home or a child or a ministry so much that we become consumed and stop yearning for God, we've left our first love.

For additional reflection: What are you waiting for right now? Has this desire ever preoccupied you to the point where your relationship with God became a lesser priority?

16. "The LORD will accomplish what concerns me; Your lovingkindness, O LORD, is everlasting" (Psalm 138:8a).

"Let us run with endurance the race that is set before us, looking to <u>Jesus, the founder and perfecter of our faith</u>" (Hebrews 12:1c-2a ESV).

Do you believe that God *will* accomplish what concerns you? Sometimes when a ministry opportunity passes us by, or a church treats us poorly, or we find ourselves stuck in a trial that seem inescapable, it can be easy to doubt God's plan for us will be fulfilled.

But the truth is, God is fully sovereign and His Word is absolute truth, and He is the author and finisher of our faith. (Hebrews 12:2) Since God promises that He will accomplish what concerns us, we can be convinced this is true.

We need to tell ourselves, "God is good, even though I'm still single, or even though I'm being mistreated, or even

28

though we have unpaid bills, or even though I'm not where I want to be—or whatever it is today that we are struggling with—God is good and He loves me and He is working these things in my life together for good. Even my physical health, even my limited finances, whatever I think is a limitation is not a limitation to the incredible things God has planned for me."

When we are tempted to doubt, we must remember that either God is the God He says He is or He is not God at all. There is no middle ground or leeway to create a god who sporadically cares for us, who occasionally keeps sparrows from falling to the ground, and who sometimes has enough power to answer your prayers. He will *finish and perfect* our faith.

For additional reflection: Since God is both the author and finisher of your faith, and He knows what He is doing in your life, will you rest and just trust Him? Will you let go of the feelings of disappointment and regret and self-pity and believe that God is working everything together for good in your life—and here is the most incredible part— according to His amazing plan that He wrote for you before you were even born?

17. "For I consider that the sufferings of this present time are not worthy to be compared with the glory that is to be revealed to us" (Romans 8:18).

While our suffering on earth may be heart-wrenching, somehow the life to come will far outweigh the suffering. This life, however bad it may be, cannot compare to how good heaven will be.

What are things that are not worthy to be compared to each other? Comparing ten cents to a hundred billion dollars? Seeing the name of a person versus spending a lifetime with them? Seeing a picture of the ocean versus owning a home on the shoreline? And none of these analogies are worthy to be compared with Paul's statement above.

The coming glory is so great that even the worst a person may suffer on earth will not compare. That's why Paul sought to lose his life here on earth. He tasted the eternal glory that awaited him and understood that whatever he suffered on earth was small compared to the coming glory.

But sometimes we get things mixed up. We want the satisfaction and glory of heaven now, and we want to skip the cross and the sufferings of Christ.

Yet somehow it is suffering that helps bring us nearer to the glory and joy we will have forever. "For momentary, light affliction is producing for us an eternal weight of glory far beyond all comparison" (2 Corinthians 4:17).

God does not let us suffer needlessly. Our suffering, our stress, our trouble is producing in us "a glory that vastly outweighs them and will last forever!" (2 Corinthians 4:17b NLT).

For additional reflection: How does understanding the glory to come help put your current trials in perspective?

18. "Make sure that your character is free from the love of money, being content with what you have; for He Himself has said, 'I WILL NEVER DESERT YOU, NOR WILL I EVER FORSAKE YOU'" (Hebrews 13:5).

In the Garden of Eden, Eve lived without sin. She had a husband who loved her. She had beautiful surroundings. She had all the fresh, organic fruit she could want. She had no worries about her husband desiring another woman. She didn't have to lose sleep over finances. She never agonized over an imperfect body or concerned herself with being judged by others. She had no health issues or pain to bother her. No bad relationships. No painful memories. No haunting regrets. She didn't have to worry about taxes or "getting it all done." She lacked nothing and had an abundance of everything she might want.

There was only one thing in the whole world she couldn't have. She couldn't eat fruit from the tree of the knowledge of good and evil.

So what did Eve do? She wanted that fruit! Satan deceived Eve into believing that God was withholding something from her. Even in the Garden of Eden—

paradise on earth—Eve still believed the lie that this fruit would be better and more satisfying then everything she already had.

It's interesting, isn't it? Even in the Garden of Eden, when the one living woman had all she could want, she still wanted the one thing she didn't have. She wanted a piece of fruit from the one tree that God forbid.

And don't we do the same thing? Just like Eve, we want the things we don't have. Instead of being satisfied by all God richly gives us, we want more. Eve thought she would be better off if she ate the forbidden fruit. It would make her "wise," the fruit was so beautiful, and it would taste so good. Yet death came to her instead.

You see, like God commanded Eve not to eat the fruit, He commands us to be content with what we have. (Hebrews 13:5) When we doubt God, we show that we don't believe God is enough—and we foolishly believe there is something better that God is withholding from us. Like Eve, we think we know better than God because we believe He is withholding good things from us.

Because Eve doubted God's goodness, she also doubted that God knew best when He instructed her to not eat the fruit. And so she broke God's command because she didn't believe that God knew best.

We need to believe God is good so we can be content with what He gives us.

For additional reflection: When you don't have something you really want, are you more likely to doubt that God is loving enough or powerful enough to give it to you?

19. "I will give thanks to You, for I am fearfully and wonderfully made; wonderful are Your works, and my soul knows it very well. My frame was not hidden from You, when I was made in secret, and skillfully wrought in the depths of the earth" (Psalm 139:14-15).

This phrase, "wonderfully made," from Psalm 139:14, is translated from the Hebrew word "Palah" meaning "to be distinct, marked out, be separated, be distinguished". In other words, God uniquely formed you in your mother's womb, distinguishing you from all of His other works. You are distinct from all other people who have ever lived or will ever live because you have been carefully created by God.

The phrase "intricately woven" or "skillfully wrought" in verse 15 speaks of needlework, the skillful masterpiece of an embroiderer. God shaped you in the womb individually and skillfully. You were not just a random outcome of genetic makeup, but you were intricately woven by God.

For additional reflection: "O LORD, You have searched me and known me. You know when I sit down and when I rise up; You understand my thought from afar. You scrutinize my path and my lying down, and are intimately acquainted with all my ways. Even before there is a word on my tongue, behold, O LORD, You know it all. You have enclosed me behind and before, and laid Your hand upon me" (Psalm 139:1-5).

How does knowing that God skillfully made you and continues to devote so much care and attention to you help you trust His goodness?

20. "For the LORD God is a sun and shield; The LORD gives grace and glory; No good thing does He withhold from those who walk uprightly" (Psalm 84:11).

"What then shall we say to these things? If God is for us, who is against us? He who did not spare His own Son, but delivered Him over for us all, how will He not also with Him freely give us all things?" (Romans 8:31-32).

If something is good for us to have according to God's purpose for our lives, we will have it! If we don't have it, and we are walking uprightly, we know that it's not a "good thing" for us right now.

God's timing is far better than our timing. Like fruit in early spring, that good thing for which we wait may be unripe and premature if we had in now. But if we wait for God's perfect schedule—believing that every "fruit" God has for us will be given at the moment of exact ripeness and sweetness—we will find that the thing for which we wait we be far better for the delay.

Our preoccupation then, is to be on obeying God, trusting Him, and believing He is good. However barren the tree may look now, the fruit will be worth the waiting!

For additional reflection: What are some things that you might want but don't have right now? How might they not be "good things" for you at this specific season in your life?

Reflections 21–30 ~ Believing that God

is Sovereign

21. "Your eyes have seen my unformed substance; and <u>in</u> <u>Your book were all written the days that were ordained</u> <u>for me, when as yet there was not one of them</u>" (Psalm 139:16).

"He made from one man every nation of mankind to live on all the face of the earth, <u>having determined their</u> <u>appointed times and the boundaries of their habitation</u>" (Acts 17:26).

Has there ever been a time in your life when so many different parts, all seeming to be random, suddenly fit together perfectly and you realized God was at work the whole time? And suddenly it becomes impossible that every detail happened by chance?

When we remember that God has pre-determined our days, this means God knows and He sees your trials and heartbreaks. God knows if you've been struggling in your marriage and feel ready to give up. He sees the things you're frustrated with, your struggles, and your anxieties. He knows if you're stressed about money or your job or your health or your children, and He knows what the outcome of the situation will be.

He's already written tomorrow and the next day and the next in His book. God isn't waiting to invent a solution to your problem—He already knows the result of your every trial. And God is aware of any sin or habit in your life you feel you can't overcome. God already knew all these things before He ever made you.

And when He made you, you were formed exactly how you needed to be formed according to what you would need for every moment and every day that God laid out for you in advance.

Your life was not an accident. Whatever the circumstances of your conception, whatever choices your parents made, whatever brought you onto this earth,

God ordained your life. He planned when you would be born and every day you would live.

Now some people might wonder, how do our choices fit in with God's plan? Here's the thing. God is proactive in our lives. While we make decisions and do what we want, God is at work all the while moving things according to His will.

So did God plan your sin? He does not ordain sin, but somehow He is able to write the story of a life that will glorify Him in the midst of our sin. That can only be God's work. If God did not pre-determine our lives, the good works we would do, and the way we might glorify Him on earth, I'm sure we would irrecoverably mess things up.

At the crucifixion of Jesus, we see man's choice and God's will intersect perfectly. The exact day was predicted by Daniel. But what if on that day, the chief priests and Pilate and the soldiers decided that Jesus was a great guy? What if they chose to wait a little longer and not crucify Him just yet? Were they not free to make those sort of decisions?

But the Bible says that "this Man, delivered over by <u>the predetermined plan and foreknowledge of God</u>, you nailed to a cross by the hands of godless men and put Him to death" (Acts 2:23). How could God guarantee that the hearts of these men would want to kill His Son on the exact day He predicted? If God knew it in advance, were they no longer free to make any other decision? So you may say, "Well, God knew what they were going to do." But the Bible doesn't just say that God knew but that He predetermined the plan. He knew the plan, yes. But He *wrote* the plan. And in writing the plan, God guaranteed it would happen.

So in your life, God has pre-written the plan. Now, this does not negate our freedom to make decisions and be fully accountable to them. Rather, it gives us the confidence to know that God really will do an amazing work in our lives.

For additional reflection: What goes through your mind when you think about how God has written all the days you will live in His book? If you could see God's master plan for your life—beginning to end, the hidden mysteries and unnoticed miracles—how would that change what you do and think today?

22. "So I say to you, ask, and it will be given to you; seek, and you will find; knock, and it will be opened to you" (Luke 11:9).

God has limitless power and nothing is too hard for Him. So why doesn't He act more quickly? Why did Nehemiah need to fast and pray for four months before approaching the king to rebuild the wall in Jerusalem? Why did Daniel fast and pray for three weeks while waiting to hear a response from God? Why is there any delay when God is all-powerful and knows all things and loves us so much?

One reason why God doesn't answer more quickly can be illustrated by a recent experience with my son James. A couple days ago he brought in the mail. On the cover of the ad pages was a large advertisement for an after-school daycare program with bowling, cooking classes, art stations, and bright fun looking rooms. James asked me, "Mom, can I please do this? Please can we go here? I want to go here so bad."

So I called to find out how much it would cost for James to go play there a few times. I was told I would need to come in to find out the prices, which meant they would be expensive. But I decided to go in and find out, hoping that James' curiosity would be satisfied by seeing the place in person and it would curb his desire to go.

Because I don't need a daycare—my kids don't even leave the house for school most days (being homeschooled)—this would be purely a luxury expense. And a big one too. But since I knew I would be close to the daycare for another errand later that afternoon, I made an appointment and we took the tour.

After leaving (and knowing the prices), I asked James how much he wanted this. Did he want it in place of Christmas presents? What would he sacrifice or give up to go there? I decided I would wait and see how often he asked. If he began to pray for this every night, I would know he really wanted it and we would see if this was a realistic option. If he excitedly mentioned it multiple times each day, prayed for it every night, and told all his friends and relatives, and continued this for months on end, I would probably sacrifice half of my grocery budget for a month just to buy it for him. The more I knew he wanted it, the more likely I would give it to him.

Jesus says the same thing in Luke 11:9-10. "So I say to you, ask, and it will be given to you; seek, and you will find; knock, and it will be opened to you. For everyone who asks, receives; and he who seeks, finds; and to him who knocks, it will be opened".

In the original Greek language, the word "ask" is αἰτέω, which is transliterated as aiteō. This word also means "beg, call for, crave, desire, require." Additionally, based on the context of this passage, this word does not mean simply "ask just one time and you will get it" but "ask and then keep on asking with great persistence and importunity." Make repeated requests to the point of being annoying.

The NLT version says it this way: "And so I tell you, keep on asking, and you will receive what you ask for. Keep on seeking, and you will find. Keep on knocking, and the door will be opened to you" (Luke 11:9 NLT).

Though James would still love to go, he understands that it costs a huge amount of money and there are other things he would want more. So he stopped asking after the first day and it was easy for us to move on.

But when we really want something, what are we willing to do to have it? Have you earnestly, persistently, fervently asked your Father in heaven? Have you fasted and prayed about these things?

Fasting shows we want it. When I fast about something, I'm serious about it.

We also must remember there is an unseen spiritual dimension to what we see on earth. We do not wrestle against flesh and blood. "For our struggle is not against flesh and blood, but against the rulers, against the powers, against the world forces of this darkness, against the spiritual forces of wickedness in the heavenly places" (Ephesians 6:12).

Prayer *with fasting* gives us greater victory over the spiritual forces of evil.

For additional reflection: Have you prayed with fasting in the past for a specific person or issue? Was there any

45

difference in the intensity or speed of that answer compared to things you have prayed about without fasting?

23. "All the inhabitants of the earth are accounted as nothing, but He does according to His will in the host of heaven and among the inhabitants of earth; and no one can ward off His hand or say to Him, 'What have You done?'" (Daniel 4:35).

God works all things according to "the counsel of His will." God chooses what He wants to happen and when they will happen—and then they happen. He is involved in causing all things to work together in a way that causes His purpose to be accomplished.

"[In Him] also we have obtained an inheritance, having been predestined according to His purpose <u>who works all things after the counsel of His will</u>" (Ephesians 1:11).

Believing that God is Sovereign

Whatever God wants to do, He is able to do. This means, God can do anything that is according to His will and His nature. Because Jesus is the exact representation of the nature of God, we see that God does not exercise His power like a tyrant, but rather that God loves us so much He would die in our place. He loves us so much that He would sacrificially suffer on a cross, share His eternal inheritance, and love us forever. He just also happens to be able to do anything.

Everything God wants to do aligns with His character, and His character of love, goodness, compassion, grace, sovereignty, and wisdom will never change. J.C. Ryle said, "Faith never rests so calmly and peacefully as when it lays its head on the pillow of God's omnipotence."[1] There is never a request we will ask of God that is too difficult for Him to answer.

"Ah Lord GOD! Behold, You have made the heavens and the earth by Your great power and by Your outstretched arm! Nothing is too difficult for You" (Jeremiah 32:17).

Every painful storm in life passes through God's knowledge—and not only that—but as the author and perfecter of our faith, the storms are never more than we can handle and never less than what we need.

For additional reflection: What attribute of God—His sovereignty, goodness, wisdom, or power—do you most struggle to believe?

Which attribute is easiest for you to believe? Why do you think it is easy for you to believe this attribute?

24. "The mystery which has been hidden from the past ages and generations, but has now been manifested to His saints, to whom God willed to make known what is the riches of the glory of <u>this mystery</u> among the Gentiles, <u>which is Christ in you, the hope of glory</u>" (Colossians 1:26-27).

"For those whom He foreknew, <u>He also predestined to become conformed to the image of His Son</u>, so that He would be the firstborn among many brethren" (Romans 8:29).

Even when we suffer, God is still orchestrating and allowing the events in our lives because they are needed for the masterpiece He is creating—which is Christ in us, the hope of glory—because God is making us into the glorious likeness of Christ.

A chisel is needed to make a beautiful marble sculpture, yet the hammer and chisel in the hands of a master artist produces a breathtaking work of art. So God uses the pain of trials as a chisel in the work of art He is making.

Some people believe it's not God's plan for us to suffer, but the Bible says otherwise. Just as it was God's purpose for Christ to suffer, suffering is still part of the Christian life:

"If children, heirs also, heirs of God and fellow heirs with Christ, if indeed we suffer with Him so that we may also be glorified with Him" (Romans 8:17).

"Now I rejoice in what I am suffering for you, and I fill up in my flesh what is still lacking in regard to Christ's afflictions, for the sake of his body, which is the church" (Colossians 1:24 NIV).

49

Some people believe that God powerlessly weeps with us and has no power to stop the bad things that happen. They believe that because God allows us to make choices, He has given up His power and no longer has any influence over what happens on earth. The problem with this idea is that it contradicts a huge amount of Scripture. Verses like "There is no wisdom, no insight, no plan that can succeed against the LORD" (Proverbs 21:30 NIV) show us that God is still the ultimate authority, even when evil seems to be winning.

Now, while God does not cause people to sin, He has the power to stop sin and sometimes He doesn't, just like He didn't stop Adam and Eve from eating the fruit in the Garden, or Cain from killing Abel, or King David from committing adultery with Bathsheba and then killing her husband.

God is not the author of evil and He does not orchestrate the evil things that happen on earth, but Satan must seek permission from God before he acts. (Job 1:6-19; 2:1-8) Somehow, though we may not understand, God allows Satan to be the ruler of this world and He permits wickedness to continue.

God has influence over all things, which means He can allow or prevent things according to His purposes and His will. So while we are "free" to make choices on earth regarding earthly things, God can change our heart, overrule our choice, kill us, or whatever He wants at anytime.

The thing is—God cares about us *so much*, He is *so concerned* about us, so intimately involved in our lives, loves us so much, is so intent on His authorship of our faith, so focused on the masterpiece He is creating that He knows what is happening and He is allowing each thing—even our bad decisions and the bad decisions of others—because they are part of the final picture, the final result of our faith.

God is not sculpting us up to our standard, but up to His standard. So while we may think a trial is unnecessary, He is a far better crafter than we.

The pain, the heartbreak, the frustrating things we've gone through—though they may not make much sense to us now—are part of the final result that will make us stand back one day and say, "WOW! I had no idea the masterpiece you were making would be this amazing, this stunning. I had no idea that the trials that made me feel unheard and alone were really part of this work of art so beyond all I could have imagined."

The earth, the intricacies of the human eye, the Grand Canyon, Niagara Falls, the vast expanse of space with its stars and black holes and unexplored galaxies, God doesn't call any of those things His masterpiece. He calls *us* His masterpiece. Let that really hit you. "For we are God's masterpiece. He has created us anew in Christ Jesus, so we can do the good things he planned for us long ago" (Ephesians 2:10).

Haven't you seen beautiful things in nature? And God made the earth in only six days. If He could make a world so amazing in six days, and He is spending much more time than that on you, and calling you His masterpiece, imagine what He is doing *in you*. And when the hammer hits the chisel, and the pain comes, remember that every tap the ultimate artist makes is perfect, and above all His creation, God calls you His *masterpiece*.

For additional reflection: Hebrews 11:1 says "Now faith is the assurance of things hoped for, the conviction of things not seen." What does it mean to have faith that you are God's masterpiece?

In what areas of your life are you most likely to lack faith, and how can you apply Hebrews 11:1 to these situations?

25. "If we are faithless, He remains faithful, for He cannot deny Himself" (2 Timothy 2:13).

"Being confident of this, that he who began a good work in you will carry it on to completion until the day of Christ Jesus" (Philippians 1:6 NIV).

God does not depend upon our correct responses to complete His work in our lives. He is always working all things together for good for those who love Him—even if we don't trust Him like we should. His goodness, sovereignty, and work in our lives is not dependent on some perfect response from us. God is God even when we doubt Him.

If we have put our faith in Jesus for salvation and we acknowledge Him as Lord of our life, then even when we fall short of living like we should, we can be confident that He will keep us in Christ.

This does not mean that a person who purposefully continues to disobey God's commands is saved, because 1 John 2:4 says, "The one who says, 'I have come to know Him,' and does not keep His commandments, is a liar, and the truth is not in him." But, when those who truly love God struggle or doubt or fall short, they can be confident that it is God's grace on their life that keeps them.

For additional reflection: According to the following verse, why do people who know God obey His commandments?

"If you love Me, you will keep My commandments" (John 14:15).

26. "<u>We give great honor to those who endure under suffering</u>. For instance, you know about Job, a man of great endurance. You can see how the Lord was kind to him at the end, for the Lord is full of tenderness and mercy" (James 5:11).

James tells us that great honor is given to those who endure under suffering. Wow. Because Job endured, because He continued to trust God, He lived to see God's kindness through tangible blessings. Even before the greatness of heaven, Job received good things from God while still on earth.

As I thought about how God rewarded Job, I realized that God continued to reward Job over a period of many years. While we read, "Job had seven sons and three daughters" etc…, they were not all born in one year. When we endure through suffering, we may continue to receive the blessings that follow for many years like Job's children continued to be born for many years after his trial ended.

And whatever honor you do or don't receive on earth, heaven will *always* be enough.

For additional reflection: "O LORD, You have searched me and known me. You know when I sit down and when I rise up; You understand my thought from afar. You scrutinize my path and my lying down, and are intimately acquainted with all my ways. Even before there is a word on my tongue, behold, O LORD, You know it all. You have enclosed me behind and before, and laid Your hand upon me" (Psalm 139:1b-5).

Based on these verses, what things does God know about us? When does God know what we say? Who goes before us and follows after us?

How does believing that God loves you and is intimately acquainted with you comfort you when life is difficult?

27. "For as high as the heavens are above the earth, *so great is His lovingkindness toward those who fear Him*...Just as a father has compassion on his children, so the LORD has compassion on those who fear Him. For He

Himself knows our frame; He is mindful that we are but dust. As for man, his days are like grass; as a flower of the field, so he flourishes. When the wind has passed over it, it is no more, and its place acknowledges it no longer. *But the lovingkindness of the LORD is from everlasting to everlasting on those who fear Him*...The LORD has established His throne in the heavens, *and His sovereignty rules over all*" (Psalm 103:11, 13-17a, 19).

When I thank God, I am acknowledging that He knows what He is doing with my life. I don't have to be anxious because I know God is my shelter and my refuge. He is not partly sovereign, kind-of-powerful, mostly good, or usually wise. He is always sovereign, always all-powerful, always good, and always wise.

Joseph experienced one devastating blow after another on his way to the position of second highest ruler of Egypt. Let's go back and look at the path Joseph traveled.

He was his father Jacob's favorite son and thus hated by his ten older brothers. They wanted to kill him but instead sold him as a slave to Midianite traders. Beside his mom, dad and younger brother Benjamin, Joseph's older brothers probably meant the world to him. He grew up with these guys and probably felt the way younger brothers feel about their older brothers. These were his *brothers*. They were not some casual acquaintances.

And when he went to visit them, they decided to *kill* him. What a horrible thing for anybody to experience. Then one brother convinces the others to sell Joseph instead of killing him. It was not as though the government or a terrorist group or some other random attacker ripped Joseph from his family, but his own brothers willingly sold him into slavery.

As a slave, Joseph worked for a man named Potiphar who eventually put Joseph in charge of all he owned. But, Potiphar's wife began to like Joseph too much and he fled from her advances. As a result, she accused Joseph of trying to sleep with her and he was put in prison.

Joseph likely felt discouraged while he spent two years in prison for a crime he didn't commit. But what came next would make up for the years of discouragement. Joseph's gift of interpreting dreams brought him before the king and he was appointed the second ruler in all of Egypt.

He wasn't released from prison so he could then work his way "up the ladder." But while Joseph sat in prison—seeing nothing but prison bars and a totally hopeless situation, God had already planned his immediate ascension to a position of great power and prominence.

"Until the time that [Joseph's] word came to pass, the word of the LORD tested him" (Psalm 105:19). Until Joseph was able to prove his ability to interpret dreams, he suffered in prison. During that time, the LORD tested Joseph and refined his character. The word "tested" from Psalm 105 means "to smelt, refine, test."

Isaiah 48:10 uses the same word: "Behold, I have refined you, but not as silver; I have tested you in the furnace of affliction." God also tests us, using affliction to refine us and make us more like Jesus.

It's also amazing to remember that before Joseph endured two years in prison, God told Joseph what awaited him. Joseph had dreamed the sun and moon and eleven stars—representing his father, mother, and eleven brothers—would bow down to him. Joseph knew! He knew there was something better awaiting him.

And though God hasn't told us in His Word the exact details of what will become of us on earth, we are told what will ultimately become of us. We are joint heirs with Christ! We will reign with Him! We will judge angels! (Romans 8:16-17; 2 Timothy 2:12; 1 Corinthians 6:3)

Like Joseph, we will immediately move from a place of suffering and hardship into a place of authority and great joy and acceptance.

All the time that Joseph suffered, he could not see what God was doing. Yet as we look back at his story now, we see so obviously that God was with him, that God was sovereignly working everything together to put Joseph in the exact position He wanted him to be in.

For additional reflection: Why do you think God finds it so necessary to refine us like silver?

What biblical truth about your eternal future helps you find peace during times of testing on earth?

28. "Yes, I know that in the integrity of your heart you have done this, <u>and I also kept you from sinning against Me; therefore I did not let you touch her</u>" (Genesis 20:6).

Because we know that God influences and directs all things toward His will to accomplish His purposes, we can rejoice that He is able to keep us from sinning according to His perfect will.

In the Old Testament, there are two similar stories about Abraham asking his wife Sarah to lie. Here's what happened in one of those stories. Abraham and Sarah moved to Gerar, the town where Abimelech, the king of the Philistines, lived. But Abraham feared the king would kill him and take Sarah as his wife because of her beauty, so Abraham lied and said she was his sister. Thinking Sarah was single, the king had her brought to him.

So Sarah lived somewhere on the king's property but he never pursued a relationship with her. However, as time went by, Abimelech's wife and his maids realized that none of them were getting pregnant.

Then God appeared to Abimelech in a dream and told him that Sarah was married. Abimelech responded that he took her innocently, having no idea she was married. God confirmed this, saying, "Yes, I know that in the integrity of your heart you have done this, and <u>I also kept you from sinning against Me; therefore I did not let you touch her</u>" (Genesis 20:6).

Pause for a minute and think this through. Why didn't Abimelech sleep with Sarah? He certainly could have slept with Sarah when she came to be his wife, because as far as he knew, she was a beautiful, single woman whose brother had agreed to her marriage. And he wanted Sarah. He had her brought to him. But God *did not let him touch her*. That means, God has the power and authority over people to keep them from sinning in certain ways as He sees fit.

Now God does not stop us from sinning all the time as you likely know. I certainly do! The story of Abimelech and Sarah is the very rare exception. But I've mentioned this story to emphasize that God may have kept you or others in your life from specific sins in the past, maybe even in ways that are unknown to you.

For additional reflection: In book of Hosea, God instructs Hosea to marry a prostitute named Gomer. His marriage to Gomer would be a prophecy to the Israelites of their unfaithfulness and God's continuing love.

By chapter two, Gomer has already left Hosea to chase her lovers. Hosea then prophecies of God's relationship with Israel, "<u>She will pursue her lovers, but she will not overtake them</u>; and <u>she will seek them, but will not find them</u>. Then she will say, 'I will go back to my first husband, for it was better for me then than now!'" (Hosea 2:7)

In the above verses, how does God cause His people to return to Him when they are determined to commit idolatry? Has God ever closed a door in your life that would have led to sin?

29. "Remember the former things long past, for I am God, and there is no other; I am God, and there is no one like Me, declaring the end from the beginning, and from ancient times things which have not been done, saying,

'My purpose will be established, and I will accomplish all My good pleasure'; calling a bird of prey from the east, the man of My purpose from a far country. Truly I have spoken; truly I will bring it to pass. I have planned it, surely I will do it" (Isaiah 46:9-11).

"But He answered them, 'My Father is working until now, and I Myself am working'" (John 5:17).

God does what He knows is best for His glory and our good—always. We may not be able to understand or know the specific reasons why, but we can know the chief reasons—God's glory and our good—and trust God, knowing He is involved in even the smallest details of our lives. Because of God's providence, God will do what He has purposed to do. God is always at work bringing to pass what He has planned.

This does not mean God causes anyone to sin, but that in every detail God is working to bring about His ultimate purposes. When we stress over those small details of life, forgetting that God has promised to take care of us, we will miss out on enjoying the rest He offers.

Believing that God is Sovereign

The more you trust God and stop worrying about all the things you want to change, the more you will be able to enjoy life now just the way it is. If God takes care of birds (and He does!), He will certainly take care of you.

"For this reason I say to you, do not be worried about your life, as to what you will eat or what you will drink; nor for your body, as to what you will put on. Is not life more than food, and the body more than clothing?...So do not worry about tomorrow; for tomorrow will care for itself. Each day has enough trouble of its own" (Matthew 6:25, 34).

For additional reflection: Can you think of a time in your past when you intensely worried about something? What can you learn from that experience?

Did you see God at work in your life more clearly after the situation ended? In other words, could you see afterward why God might have allowed it to happen?

30. "I know that You can do all things, and that no purpose of Yours can be thwarted...Therefore I have declared that which I did not understand, things too wonderful for me, which I did not know...Therefore I retract, and I repent in dust and ashes." (Job 42:2,3b,6).

When we don't know what God is doing, we must trust that *He knows* what He is doing. The story of Job reminds us that what God does is often beyond what we can understand, and that instead of challenging God's wisdom, it is our wisest action to humbly trust Him.

When Job suffered immeasurably, losing all his children and possessions in one day, and then getting a horrible, painful condition that caused his body to be covered in boils, he immediately fell to the ground and worshipped the Lord, saying, "Naked I came from my mother's womb, and naked I shall return there. The LORD gave and the LORD has taken away. Blessed be the name of the LORD" (Job 1:21).

That is an amazing, admirable response. Job did not accuse God of wrongdoing or question God's character. He worshipped God even though his life fell apart.

But as the days wore on, and the pain did not lessen, and his wealth did not return, and the suffering didn't subside—Job grew weary. He wondered why he was ever born, saying, "I loathe my own life; I will give full vent to my complaint; I will speak in the bitterness of my soul…Why then have You brought me out of the womb? Would that I had died and no eye had seen me! I should have been as though I had not been, carried from womb to tomb" (Job 10:1,18-19). The unceasing suffering made Job wish he had never been born. He hated his life and questioned why God allowed him to exist.

After Job's friends unsuccessfully attempted to comfort him, God addressed their mistaken ideas about Him. Rather than answering Job's questions, God questioned Job instead. God asked Job about biology, zoology, astronomy and other subjects. He asked Job, "Have you entered into the springs of the sea or walked in the recesses of the deep?" (Job 38:16). In other words, "Do you know what is at the bottom of the ocean, in the deepest cracks and trenches?" Only in the last sixty years have we even developed the technology to explore the ocean depths, so Job would have no answer to this question.

God also asked Job about his power over nature. "Can you send forth lightnings that they may go and say to you, 'Here we are'?" (Job 38:35). Since Job did not have power over lightning storms, again he would have to admit that he didn't know how God worked.

God's questions revealed to Job that there was so much he didn't know, so much of God's wisdom and understanding and ways that were beyond Job's comprehension. Though Job may not have understood specifically why God allowed him to suffer, Job did begin to understand God's greatness.

Job responded to God's questions by saying, "I know that You can do all things, and that no purpose of Yours can be thwarted...Therefore I have declared that which I did not understand, things too wonderful for me, which I did not know...Therefore I retract, and I repent in dust and ashes." (Job 42:2,3b,6).

To explain the depth of these verses, I would rather quote those who are far more eloquent than myself.

"Job's confession and repentance took place finally. He still did not know why he suffered so profoundly, but he was done complaining, questioning, and challenging God's wisdom and justice. He was reduced to such utter humility, crushed beneath the weight of God's greatness, that all he could do was repent for his insolence. Without answers to all of his questions, Job quietly bowed in humble submission before his Creator and admitted that God was sovereign. Most importantly for the message of the book, Job was still diseased and without his children and possessions, and God had not changed anything (except for the humbling of the heart of His servant)." (John MacArthur, MacArthur Study Bible NASB Job 42)

Commentator Matthew Henry says, "We see what God does, but we neither know why he does it, what he is aiming at, nor what he will bring it to. These are things too wonderful for us, out of our sight to discover, out of our reach to alter, and out of our jurisdiction to judge of. They are things which we know not; it is quite above our capacity to pass a verdict upon them. The reason why we quarrel with Providence is because we do not understand it; and we must be content to be in the dark about it, until the mystery of God shall be finished." (Blue Letter Bible, www.blb.org, Matthew Henry Commentary, Job 42)

For additional reflection: Job endured some of the most difficult things we can face as humans. What was Job's response?

Read Job 38-42. Choose a couple of the verses from these chapters that speak to you and write them down. Mark what you like about each verse.

Reflections 31–40 ~ Trusting God in Difficult Times

31. "The LORD is my rock and my fortress and my deliverer, my God, my rock, in whom I take refuge; my shield and the horn of my salvation, my stronghold." (Psalm 18:2).

"But I am afflicted and needy; hasten to me, O God! You are my help and my deliverer; O LORD, do not delay" (Psalm 70:5).

This may be a season of suffering and difficulty for you, but God made a world where the seasons change. God is called the Deliverer because He has the power to save you and rescue you. He is able to deliver you from whatever you are enduring.

Even if we think of the worst things a person can suffer on earth, we must remember that this is the worst it will ever get for those who will spend eternity with God. For those who will be separated from God eternally, this life is the best it will ever get.

"For I consider that the sufferings of this present time are not worthy to be compared with the glory that is to be revealed to us" (Romans 8:18).

For additional reflection: What do you want God to deliver you from? How can understanding this life is the worst it will ever get bring you comfort?

32. "Paul, a bond-servant of God and an apostle of Jesus Christ, <u>for the faith of those chosen of God</u> and the knowledge of the truth which is according to godliness" (Titus 1:1).

Our faith is God's big priority. Paul said he was a bond slave of God and an apostle of Jesus Christ—in part—for the faith of those chosen of God. Paul had to suffer that our faith might be strengthened.

God wants us to be strong in faith, to believe fully in Him, and to keep growing in the degree that we trust Him and depend on Him. From my view, trials seem to be a quick way to intensify that process.

Remember that it is in hard times and painful seasons that we learn to trust God more and depend on Him. When we trust God, we are willing to give up what others have and what we could still have—because we know the value of following Jesus is far greater than anything else we might gain.

The key to trusting God is remembering <u>Who</u> we are trusting in, remembering that God has the power to save us, deliver us, help us, direct us, encourage us, comfort us, protect us, empower us, strengthen us, and give us faith. This trust is a dependent, childlike faith that looks to God and believes He is able and willing to help.

And then it's a faith that knows whatever happens, whatever faith we had, whatever good was done, the glory and the praise belong to God, for He was always working and always caring and always conforming us into the image of Christ.

When we trust God, it is only because God makes us able to trust Him. Thankfulness and contentment are God's work in us. Therefore, all the glory for our obedience, for our faith, for our thankfulness, belongs to God.

"For it is God who is at work in you, both to will and to work for His good pleasure" (Philippians 2:13).

For additional reflection: Is there anything in your life that you need to release to God? How would you fill in the blanks in the following sentence: I have a hard time trusting God when _____, but I believe that God is at work in me.

However you feel about your calling, your gifts, and your situation in life, remember you are God's work.

Dear Lord, you are the One at work in me. I release my gifts to you, my opportunities, my failures, my successes. I know that You are working in me for Your good pleasure.

33. "But by the grace of God I am what I am, and His grace toward me did not prove vain; but I labored even more than all of them, yet not I, but the grace of God with me" (1 Corinthians 15:10).

Just because we trust God does not mean we sit back and do nothing. We must trust *and* obey. There are three ways we can trust and obey God during times of waiting for His deliverance.

First, get wisdom! What have other godly and wise people done in your situation? What strategies might help with the trial you are in? If you don't know, search out the answer. "The beginning of wisdom is: Acquire wisdom; and with all your acquiring, get understanding" (Proverbs 4:7). Get counsel from wise and godly people because "where there is no guidance the people fall, but in abundance of counselors there is victory" (Proverbs 11:14).

Second, pray your heart out! "The prayer of a righteous person is powerful and effective" (James 5:16 NIV). "The eyes of the LORD are toward the righteous and His ears are open to their cry" (Psalm 34:15).

Third, take action. Do what you can according to what is wise and pleasing to God. And work your hardest because there are promises for diligence. "Do you see a man skilled [diligent, quick, prompt, ready] in his work? He will stand before kings; He will not stand before obscure men" (Proverbs 22:29).

For additional reflection: Have you ever felt upset because you wanted something and God didn't give it to you (or still hasn't given it to you)?

What can you do as you wait for God's answer?

34.   "I am the man who has seen affliction because of the rod of His wrath. He has driven me and made me walk in darkness and not in light...In dark places He has made me dwell, like those who have long been dead. He has walled me in so that I cannot go out; He has made my chain heavy" (Lamentations 3:1-2, 6-7).

During the trial from which this book was born, I remember feeling that I was in a tunnel, but there was no light at the end of it and I would be stuck there forever. Maybe you have felt like that also.

Throughout the first couple years of that trial, it was bearable. But somehow it grew heavier, harder as the years wore by. I think that was because my hope for change or deliverance had diminished. I would say to the Lord, "There is no way out." And I believe that. There was no *human* way out. I felt like Jeremiah, and God had made me dwell in dark places without light or escape. Things continued to get worse as time went by. And because of the stress, my health went downhill.

As Jeremiah said, so I felt, "My strength has perished, and so has my hope from the LORD" (Lamentations 3:18). I knew my hope and my deliverance would come because I knew I would see my Savior's face and be with Him forever. But seeing deliverance while still on earth? I wasn't so convinced.

But then, in light of his suffering, Jeremiah goes on to say, "Why should any living mortal, or any man, offer complaint in view of his sins?" (Lamentations 3:39).

77

Though Jeremiah suffered greatly, He understood how amazing it is that we have not already received eternal judgment because we have sinned so greatly against God. What's amazing is that we have anything wonderful in this life at all. While we deserve eternal judgment, we have received grace upon grace.

While God could give us lives on earth that represent the fullness of His anger toward sin, Jeremiah says, "For if He causes grief, then He will have compassion according to His abundant lovingkindness. For He does not afflict willingly or grieve the sons of men" (Lamentations 3:32-33). While Jeremiah felt as though God's hand was against Him, he knew that God was full of lovingkindness.

"This I recall to my mind, therefore I have hope. The LORD'S lovingkindnesses indeed never cease, for His compassions never fail. They are new every morning; great is Your faithfulness. 'The LORD is my portion,' says my soul, 'Therefore I have hope in Him.' The LORD is good to those who wait for Him, to the person who seeks Him" (Lamentations 3:21-25).

Though I didn't know if it was God's will to ever deliver me, I continued to pray. And then it happened. In about a three month time period, God changed multiple situations and delivered me from the trial. The burden lifted and even my health problems went into remission.

For additional reflection: How do Jeremiah's words help you remember the greatness of God's mercy and grace toward you?

35. "But you, are you seeking great things for yourself? Do not seek them" (Jeremiah 45:5).

I don't remember the exact year when this verse penetrated my heart and shook my idea of godliness and life. But I remember how strongly it hit me. I felt as though God asked me directly, "Katie, are *you* seeking great things for yourself?" And at that moment, I saw that misguided motives and selfish ambition had a place in my heart.

My desire for great things was not necessarily evident in my day to day actions, but I knew that my heart wanted to be recognized, to be noticed as a godly woman, to be important. My heart longed for great things. I wanted to transform the world for Jesus, to live radically for him, but *I* wanted to do it. I somehow equated "great things" with "godliness." And the greater the things I did, the better I believed I would be as a Christian.

And I wonder how Baruch felt when God spoke this question through Jeremiah the prophet. Baruch was a scribe who worked with Jeremiah, transcribing the words Jeremiah dictated as he heard from the LORD. Baruch also read these prophecies in the house of the LORD. (Jeremiah 36)

So while he wasn't as famous as Jeremiah, he was Jeremiah's right hand man. He heard the words of God Jeremiah spoke before anyone. And he was on the right team. He wasn't a false prophet condemned by God, but a man directly serving God while most of Israel had strayed from Him.

So Jeremiah prophesied and Baruch wrote it all down, and he heard God's messages for the nations. But then in Jeremiah 45, suddenly the message was for *him*. God was talking *directly to him.*

First, God begins by reminding Baruch of something he had previously said: "You said, 'I am overwhelmed with trouble! <u>Haven't I had enough pain already? And now the LORD has added more!</u> I am worn out from sighing and can find no rest'" (Jeremiah 45:3 NLT).

Baruch was worn out from suffering. He felt the pain of persecution along with Jeremiah, and things weren't easy. Even today we can relate to Baruch's frustration as trials come and we wear down.

God saw Baruch's pain and cared enough about him to answer. God first told Baruch about His plans for the country. But then He says, "'But you, are you seeking great things for yourself? Do not seek them; for behold, I am going to bring disaster on all flesh,' declares the LORD, 'but I will give your life to you as booty in all the places where you may go'" (Jeremiah 45:5).

Maybe we would expect words of pure comfort. We might think that God would remind Baruch to trust Him. But instead, God cuts to Baruch's heart.

And God has cut to my heart with these words. Have I been expecting to not suffer? Have I become focused on greatness and forgot the instructions to become the servant of all?

God doesn't guarantee me fame. He doesn't guarantee me earthly success. He doesn't guarantee me greatness here on earth. But He has let me stay alive. He has given me my life.

And so I must remember that instead of seeking great things, I must be thankful for the things He's already given me, starting with my life. I am still alive here on earth, and even more importantly, I have life in Him that will last forever.

"But seek first the kingdom of God and his righteousness, and all these things will be added to you" (Matthew 6:33 ESV).

For additional reflection: What does it mean to you to "seek great things for yourself"? In what ways do you find yourself trying to earn the favor or approval of others? How can this damage your relationship with Christ?

36. "If I regard wickedness in my heart, the Lord will not hear" (Psalm 66:18).

"Then they will cry out to the LORD, but He will not answer them. Instead, He will hide His face from them at that time because they have practiced evil deeds" (Micah 3:4).

"You ask and do not receive, because you ask with wrong motives, so that you may spend it on your pleasures" (James 4:3).

These verses are a little overwhelming, but they are not the end of the story. The sins we've done in the past—if we've confessed and repented—are removed by Christ through His blood. If we are in Christ by faith, we have been reconciled to God and we can come boldly to His throne of grace. Our past forgiven sins do not keep God from hearing our prayers today.

But sometimes we may desire things that are based on wrong motives. And sometimes, God does not answer prayer because our prayer may be to avoid the discipline that God is giving to us because He loves us.

In Exodus 17, the Israelites whined and complained to have water and God told Moses to strike a specific rock. When Moses hit the rock, water came out.

The second time the Israelites asked for water, God told Moses to speak to the rock and it would bring forth water. (Numbers 20) Instead, because of his anger toward the Israelites, Moses hit the rock twice instead of speaking. When Moses disobeyed God by striking the rock, God said Moses would not go with the Israelites into the promised land.

After a long forty years, the time came to finally cross over the Jordan and enter this promised land. Moses says he *pleaded* with the Lord to cross over and see the hill country and Lebanon. But God did not change His mind or relieve Moses of this consequence. God told Moses to go to the top of Pisgah and from there he would be able to see the land, but he would never enter it.

We see another unanswered prayer in the life of David. When David committed adultery with Bathsheba, she became pregnant. After David could not get Bathsheba's husband to sleep with her, David ordered him to be killed.

After he died, David married Bathsheba and she gave birth to the child. David continued to keep his sin hidden until God sent Nathan the prophet. David confessed his sin and asked God for forgiveness, but as a consequence, the child would die.

The child became very sick and David fasted, wept, and laid all night on the ground praying that God would keep his child alive. Imagine the grief of knowing your child would die because of your sin. My heart aches even thinking about it now.

The one thing that comforts me in this story is David's words, "I will go to him, but he will not return to me" (2 Samuel 12:23). David would see his child again. Even Moses got to stand in the promised land when he appeared with Jesus on the Mount of Transfiguration.

At the time they prayed, the answer was "no". This was not a "God can't hear you because of your sin" but a direct and specific response to a specific sin.

But while God answered no in the short term, David still would be with his child in eternity, and Moses still got to enter the promised land with Jesus. That's amazing. Even in their punishments, God was still gracious. It's amazing to think that when God says "no," there may be an eternal "yes" waiting for us, and that "no" may just mean "not now."

For additional reflection: Have you ever prayed something and are now thankful that God didn't answer that prayer?

37. "There is no wisdom and no understanding and no counsel against the LORD" (Proverbs 21:30).

A friend of mine went to a faith healer many years ago seeking help for a crippling disease. When my friend wasn't healed, the faith healer proclaimed that my friend did not have enough faith. At the time, he didn't understand the Bible well enough to discern the false teaching of the faith healer.

Unanswered prayer is not an automatic indicator of sin or a lack of faith. With great distress and grief, Jesus understood that He was about to suffer and die for the sins of the world. He prayed "My Father, if it is possible, let this cup pass from Me; yet not as I will, but as You will" (Matthew 26:39).

God's did not take the cup of suffering from Jesus, and we know that because Jesus died for our sin, we will spend eternity with Him. Read just a few of things Jesus had to suffer. "After having Jesus scourged, he handed Him over to be crucified...They stripped Him and put a scarlet robe on Him. And after twisting together a crown of thorns, they put it on His head, and a reed in His right hand; and they knelt down before Him and mocked Him, saying, 'Hail, King of the Jews!' They spat on Him, and took the reed and began to beat Him on the head...And those passing by were hurling abuse at Him, wagging their heads...Then they spat in His face and beat Him with their fists; and others slapped Him" (Matthew 27:26,28-30,39,67).

"Then Pilate had Jesus flogged with a lead-tipped whip... They nailed him to the cross. Two others were crucified with him, one on either side, with Jesus between them" (John 19:1,18 NLT).

87

Though Jesus prayed for the cup of suffering and death to be removed, the will of God the Father was done and Jesus needed to die a painful and humiliating death on a cross. Sometimes God's will is different than our desires and no amount of faith or lack of faith can overrule what God plans.

"This is the confidence which we have before Him, that, if we ask anything according to His will, He hears us. And if we know that He hears us in whatever we ask, we know that we have the requests which we have asked from Him" (1 John 5:14-15). We don't always know God's will until after we've prayed. And sometimes the things we desire are not God's will.

Which takes us back to the words of Jesus, "Nevertheless, not as I will, but your will be done." Faith in God is crucial. It is the key to having a relationship with God and knowing Him. But when we don't see God's answer to our prayers, we must also have enough faith in God to say, "Your will be done."

For additional reflection: "I would have despaired unless I had believed that I would see the goodness of the LORD in the land of the living. Wait for the LORD; be strong and let your heart take courage; yes, wait for the LORD" (Psalm 27:13-14).

Has it ever been hard to believe you will see God's goodness while you are alive? What might God be teaching you in those times when His answer seems to be "no"?

38. "But [Elijah] went a day's journey into the wilderness, and came and sat down under a juniper tree; and he requested for himself that he might die, and said, 'It is enough; now, O LORD, take my life, for I am not better than my fathers.' He lay down and slept under a juniper tree; and behold, there was an angel touching him, and he said to him, 'Arise, eat.'" (1 Kings 19:4-5).

Elijah felt such great stress that he would have preferred death. Jesus and Paul also spoke of a sadness and anguish that neared death.

"Then [Jesus] said to them, 'My soul is deeply grieved, to the point of death; remain here and keep watch with Me.' And He went a little beyond them, and fell on His face and prayed, saying, 'My Father, if it is possible, let this cup pass from Me; yet not as I will, but as You will'" (Matthew 26:38-39).

Paul wrote to the Corinthians: "For we do not want you to be unaware, brethren, of our affliction which came to us in Asia, that we were burdened excessively, beyond our strength, so that we despaired even of life; indeed, we had the sentence of death within ourselves so that we would not trust in ourselves, but in God who raises the dead" (2 Corinthians 1:8-9).

I'm comforted to know that even Jesus and Paul and Elijah have felt sadness so great that it could have killed them. Therefore I know that it's not the feeling of despair that is sin, but the response.

When faced with feelings of grief to the point of death, Jesus said, "Nevertheless, not as I will, but your will be done." Paul trusted in the God who raises the dead. And Elijah took a good nap!

For additional reflection: Have you ever felt sorrow to the point of death, like Jesus, or have you ever despaired of life like Paul or wished to die like Elijah? What was your response to those feelings?

Take a moment to pray that God will increase your faith and help you trust Him more during the hardest times in your life.

39. "We will know by this that we are of the truth, and will assure our heart before Him in whatever our heart condemns us; for God is greater than our heart and knows all things" (1 John 3:19-20).

A couple years ago I was diagnosed with having an ulcer in my small intestine. I was referred to a specialist but my insurance ended before I had an opportunity to go to the appointment.

After much prayer, the ulcer went away almost overnight at the same time my very stressful circumstances changed. Other than making myself drink large amounts of raw cabbage juice, I took no prescription medicine or any other medical remedy. But the pain was gone so I believe the ulcer healed also.

Then suddenly, about two years later, a horrible pain developed in my back radiating through my stomach. The pain, which felt very similar to the ulcer I had, woke me up all night with sharp, stabbing agony.

During that time I looked online and read about how advanced ulcers can cause back pain and untreated, lead to stomach cancer. So then I had the seed planted in my mind, "What if this is stomach cancer? What if the ulcer never went away. What if my kids grow up without a mother?"

By God's grace, I think it might have been some sort of virus because it healed completely within a week. But the fear of having cancer caused me to feel so much sympathy for a friend of my sister who has cancer. Her friend has three small children—the youngest only six months old—and my sister watches the kids while the mother does her chemotherapy. And then I think of the heartbreak of knowing that if her cancer treatment is unsuccessful, the children will be left without their mother.

I have so many stories that burn in my heart—true stories of friends or relatives who've suffered indescribably because of sickness or death or abuse or suicide or adultery or many other things. And so we have a hard time believing that our God who is so powerful, and so good, could also know everything.

Because if He knows everything, He knew about the cancer and the adultery and the birth defects and the suicide and the jail time before they ever happened—and yet He didn't stop them from happening. So then we doubt God's goodness. "How can a loving God allow this kind of suffering?" so many people ask.

So we think, we'll maybe God isn't interfering with our "freewill." But then how do we explain His sovereignty and verses like, "There is no wisdom, no insight, no plan that can succeed against the LORD" (Proverbs 21:30 NIV). How is Satan allowed to take a child's mother by cancer or how was He able to take all of Job's children from him? Is it not because God's allows it?

So what would be God's purpose in allowing so much suffering? Maybe, in part, all these sufferings are meant to cause of to realize that when Paul said, "For I reckon that the sufferings of this present time are not worthy to be compared to the glory to be revealed in us," that in light of the severity of the sufferings, we might grasp just a little of the far greater magnitude of the coming glory.

"Lift up your eyes on high and see who has created these stars, the One who leads forth their host by number, He calls them all by name; because of the greatness of His might and the strength of His power, not one of them is missing" (Isaiah 40:26).

For additional reflection: One tragic example of suffering is the Sandy Hook Elementary School shooting. Twenty children and six adults died at the hands of a twenty-year old man. And I can't help but cry from the overwhelming sadness of it all. My youngest son is also seven years old, like many of the children who died, and my heart can't even imagine the grief of something so devastating.

In Jesus' time, there was also an unexpected tragedy. A tower in Siloam fell and killed eighteen people. Jesus commented on the event by saying, "Or do you suppose that those eighteen on whom the tower in Siloam fell and killed them were worse culprits than all the men who live in Jerusalem? I tell you, no, but unless you repent, you will all likewise perish" (Luke 13:4-5).

I believe that in His words, the message we must see is that because death is coming to us all, and this life is so fleeting compared to eternity, that unless we follow Christ now, a far worse suffering is still to come. I believe Jesus is reminding us that it's our eternal portion that really matters. This suffering won't last, but eternal suffering will never end.

I believe that is also why Jesus says, "Do not fear those who kill the body but are unable to kill the soul; but rather fear Him who is able to destroy both soul and body in hell" (Matthew 10:28). Because eternity will last *forever*, it is not this life we must be most concerned about. This life will pale in comparison to *forever*.

In considering what Jesus said about the tragedy of Siloam, why do you think Jesus responded the way He did? Why do you think our suffering on earth puts eternity in perspective and can help us long for our eternal home that much more?

40. "And if children, heirs also, heirs of God and fellow heirs with Christ, if indeed we suffer with Him so that we may also be glorified with Him" (Romans 8:17).

God's plan for you hasn't changed just because things have gone "wrong." His will for your life is still right where He wants it to be. Suffering here on earth is part of one day being glorified with Jesus forever.

People often have the misconception that if God loves us, He will make life easy for us. But life was not easy for His only begotten Son Jesus, who was killed by crucifixion on a cross after being beaten, whipped, accused of crimes He didn't commit, punched in the face, betrayed, mocked, and rejected.

Life was not easy for Paul the Apostle, who wrote a large number of books in the New Testament. He was beaten with rods, whipped, stoned almost to death, shipwrecked, starved, put in prison, maligned, and abandoned by his friends.

Life was not easy for the prophet Jeremiah, who was lowered into a well and left to die. Life was not easy for many of the earliest Christians, who were killed for their faith in Christ's resurrection.

An easy, happy life is not necessarily a sign of God's favor and a life of difficulty and suffering is not a sign of God's rejection.

Read what Paul wrote about the suffering he endured as a follower of Jesus: "Are they servants of Christ?—I speak as if insane—I more so; in far more labors, in far more imprisonments, beaten times without number, often in danger of death. Five times I received from the Jews thirty-nine lashes. Three times I was beaten with rods, once I was stoned, three times I was shipwrecked, a night and a day I have spent in the deep. I have been on frequent journeys, in dangers from rivers, dangers from robbers, dangers from my countrymen, dangers from the Gentiles, dangers in the city, dangers in the wilderness, dangers on the sea, dangers among false brethren; I have been in labor and hardship, through many sleepless

97

nights, in hunger and thirst, often without food, in cold and exposure" (2 Corinthians 11:23-27).

Paul also wrote: "To this present hour we are both hungry and thirsty, and are poorly clothed, and are roughly treated, and are homeless" (1 Corinthians 4:11).

We learn about some of the suffering of other believers in the book of Hebrews: "Others experienced mockings and scourgings, yes, also chains and imprisonment. They were stoned, they were sawn in two, they were tempted, they were put to death with the sword; they went about in sheepskins, in goatskins, being destitute, afflicted, ill-treated" (Hebrews 11:36-37).

If we belong to God, then we can be convinced that God loves us and is working in our life. We can be convinced that God has not failed us and we are still victorious in Christ.

"Can anything ever separate us from Christ's love? Does it mean he no longer loves us if we have trouble or calamity, or are persecuted, or hungry, or destitute, or in danger, or threatened with death? (As the Scriptures say, 'For your sake we are killed every day; we are being slaughtered like sheep.' No, despite all these things, overwhelming victory is ours through Christ, who loved us" (Romans 8:35-37 NLT).

For additional reflection: Think of Christians you know who have gone through great suffering and yet continue to experience God's joy. Do you believe their faith is stronger because of what they have suffered? Why or why not?

Reflections 41–50 ~ Becoming the

Servant of All

41. "Calling [His disciples] to Himself, Jesus said to them, 'You know that those who are recognized as rulers of the Gentiles lord it over them; and their great men exercise authority over them. But it is not this way among you, but whoever wishes to become great among you shall be your servant; and whoever wishes to be first among you shall be slave of all. For even the Son of Man did not come to be served, but to serve, and to give His life a ransom for many'" (Mark 10:42-45).

It was January, several years ago, and I got the worst stomach ache I'd ever had. It was some sort of horrible stomach virus. I could barely move because the pain and nausea were so overwhelming. But I think my immune system had become easy prey because I felt bitter and stressed almost daily. My husband watched the kids for me while I agonized over the pain up in bed.

Once I felt some relief from the pain, I began reading the poems of one of my favorite authors, Ruth Bell Graham. And it seemed as if every poem was about dying to ourselves (and all our selfish desires) and being the servant of all.

I realized that much of my stress and bitterness were really just a form of self-pity. I had been seeking to be served instead of focusing on serving others. I was performing my tasks as a wife resentfully, wishing my husband would be more considerate of me, wishing my house was easier to clean, wishing for a whole list of things over and over.

I forgot that as a Christian, I am called to pick up my cross daily and follow Jesus. I forgot it is when we sacrifice and give freely of ourselves that we most please God and find our satisfaction.

God healed both my body and my heart during that time. He allowed the sickness to refresh my heart and renew my vision for serving my family. When I focused on serving others instead of longing to be served and have an easy life, the huge weight of self-pity lifted.

For additional reflection: Do you ever think about times when you've been overlooked or mistreated and feel sorry for yourself? How can changing your focus from being served to serving others help keep your heart in the right place?

42. "To sum up, all of you be harmonious, sympathetic, brotherly, kindhearted, and humble in spirit; not returning evil for evil or insult for insult, but giving a blessing instead; for you were called for the very purpose that you might inherit a blessing" (1 Peter 3:8-9).

Replaying the wrongs people have committed against you causes you to experience them multiple times. Why suffer more than once? Instead, forget what lies behind and press on.

I'm not saying to never deal with past abuse or deep childhood pain, but in a day to day sense, if someone at church ignores you when you say "hi" to them, hope the best—that they just didn't see you because they had a lot on their mind—and then move on.

Even if the issue is more serious, and someone is critical of you and continues to put you down, or you are in a situation that is unfair, or you are continually overlooked for a job or position you really want, seek to do good instead of repaying evil.

Pray God will bless them and give them strength today for all they have to do. Pray they would remember God's love toward them. But then move on in your mind from the wrong that was done. There is no need to obsess over each time we've been overlooked or mistreated.

"Bless those who persecute you; bless and do not curse." (Romans 12:14)

Then, each time you find yourself thinking something that is not beneficial, use that negative thought as a prompt to remember to keeping praying for the very person or persons whose actions prompted that thought. Pray for them to know the truth of Christ and to experience His goodness. Pray they will repent of sin in their life and experience the refreshing that comes from time in the presence of the Lord.

For additional reflection: How can remembering these past hurts keep you from being kindhearted toward those who have hurt you?

43. "We love, because He first loved us" (1 John 4:19).

"Beloved, if God so loved us, we also ought to love one another" (1 John 4:11).

When we set up requirements which must be fulfilled in order for a person to be considered worthy of love, kindness, and honor, we have made our love conditional.

An example would be a wife who expects her husband to be godly, do family devotions, provide a reasonable income, be wise with money, be kind, and go to church— and when he falls short, she justifies withholding love, kindness, and/or honor from him as punishment. In other words, she doesn't smile at him or compliment him or admire him because she feels angry about the things he is not doing—the things she expects him to do.

Releasing your expectations to God does not mean that you no longer hold people accountable for their actions. Rather, it means you seek their good for their sake, not your own.

However, the way we are commanded to treat people is not based on how they act or what they do. God commands us to love one another and there is no "only if" clause.

The Bible doesn't say "Love your husband only if he is godly, only if he doesn't criticize you, or only if he provides for you financially." Nor does the Bible say, "Love one another only if the other person loves you first." We don't love others because they love us but because Christ first loved us.

For additional reflection: What do the following verses say about how we are to treat people?

"So, as those who have been chosen of God, holy and beloved, put on a heart of compassion, kindness, humility, gentleness and patience; bearing with one another, and forgiving each other, whoever has a complaint against anyone; just as the Lord forgave you, so also should you. Beyond all these things put on love, which is the perfect bond of unity. (Colossians 3:12-14)

"Always be humble and gentle. Be patient with each other, making allowance for each other's faults because of your love." (Ephesians 4:2 NLT).

"To sum up, all of you be harmonious, sympathetic, brotherly, kindhearted, and humble in spirit" (1 Peter 3:8).

"Not returning evil for evil or insult for insult, but giving a blessing instead; for you were called for the very purpose that you might inherit a blessing. (1 Peter 3:9).

Do any of these verses mention the way the other person must act in order to be treated this way?

44. "Therefore repent and return, so that your sins may be wiped away, in order that times of refreshing may come from the presence of the Lord" (Acts 3:19).

How blessed we are that God refreshes us Himself so we in turn can love and refresh others. We are not required to muster up strength continually for each day, but God asks us to simply come to Him and depend on Him.

If we want to have God's power and His love for us at the forefront of our memory, then we need to diligently seek Him with all our heart. We need to keep our mind saturated with the Word of God by continually meditating on Him. We need to be refreshed from our weariness by spending time with God.

For additional reflection: Since times of refreshing comes from God's presence, what are you doing to make sure you are saturated with the Word of God and time spent with Him?

45. "See to it that no one comes short of the grace of God; that no root of bitterness springing up causes trouble, and by it many be defiled" (Hebrews 12:15).

Whatever we think about is what we will end up talking about. "The good man out of the good treasure of his heart brings forth what is good; and the evil man out of the evil treasure brings forth what is evil; for his mouth speaks from that which fills his heart" (Luke 6:45).

If we let certain thoughts play through our minds unchecked, those thoughts can and will consume us until they control our behavior and direct what we say.

I have a "bitterness measure" that I use to know if I've become bitter. It started many years back, while talking to a friend about a problem she was having with her husband. She told me about some things he'd done that upset her. Then the next time I saw her, she told me the same stories again. When I saw her a few months later, she again told me the same stories about her husband, completely unaware that she'd told me those exact same stories every time I'd talked to her over the past year.

What I took away from that experience is when the same story of mistreatment is told to the same people multiple times—without the story-telling person realizing they are repeating themselves—it is the bright red warning flag of bitterness.

So when I told my husband about someone who promised to do something for me and didn't do it, he said, "I know. You already told me all that." Yikes! Right then I realized I had allowed myself to get bitter. I thought I was telling my husband for the first time what happened. But for me to tell him multiple times and not realize it meant I was thinking about this event without taking control of my thoughts. I quickly decided I would not let myself think about it again.

For additional reflection: What expectations do you have on others or on life that you may need to release to God? Are there any areas of bitterness in your heart that you need to confess and forsake?

How can placing high expectations on people keep us from walking with grace and forgiveness toward them?

46. "If anyone wants to be first, he shall be last of all and servant of all" (Mark 9:35).

"And [Jesus] was saying to them all, 'If anyone wishes to come after Me, he must deny himself, and take up his cross daily and follow Me'" (Luke 9:23).

If we think about what it means to carry a cross, we are reminded that a cross is used as a means of death. It's sort of like saying, "Carry your suicide gun." In other words, be always aware of your death. This is not a death to our physical body, but death to every part of us that might still long for the world or anything of the world. It means relinquishing any habit, craving, affection, pursuit, or activity that would keep us from living in complete obedience to God. And in light of carrying our cross, have we been willing to love, serve, and give as God leads us?

We serve others when we choose to get on our face and pray for them rather than get a little extra sleep. We serve others when we buy a gift card at the store for the person in a difficult financial position. We serve others when we notice what people are doing well and thank them for it. There are so many ways we can serve others and be less focused on ourselves.

If you are a wife, God's will is for you to love and honor your husband. So being the servant of all in marriage means serving your husband willingly, *cheerfully*, according to his preferences.

If a friend or acquaintance is distressed and you have the ability or means or wisdom to help alleviate her distress, it means you seriously consider helping as if the problem were your own. I know women who are beautiful examples of this concern for others, who bend over backwards to find and help those who most need it. I want to cry when I think of the women God has placed in my life who have served our family in times of distress.

Often, God allows us to serve others with the spiritual gifts He has given us. Which means, we get to enjoy and love serving because we are doing what we are passionate about.

Serving others does not mean that we take time away from our husband and children to help with every outside activity. "Servant of all" does not mean doormat. It never means that we forsake wisdom in the choices we make. Rather, it means that in every realm and place God has *called* us to serve, we do it wholeheartedly. It means that whatever we choose to do, being guided by wisdom, we are all-in. It means we recognize our lives belong fully to Christ.

My husband, Todd, fiercely protects my time. He knows that our family, our children, our house, even my relationship with God can all suffer if I am gone too much or if I am too overcommitted to outside activities. Through being married to Todd, I have especially learned that being a servant of all does not mean saying "yes" every time I am asked to participate or serve in something.

But denying ourselves starts with the attitude of our heart. It means humbly looking to honor and care for others instead of looking to make ourselves great.

For additional reflection: How would your life look today if you completely believed that to be great in God's kingdom you must be the servant of all? How would your attitude toward other people change, especially those closest to you?

47. "And He said to them, 'The kings of the Gentiles lord it over them; and those who have authority over them are called 'Benefactors.' But it is not this way with you, but the one who is the greatest among you must become like the youngest, and the leader like the servant. For who is greater, the one who reclines at the table or the one who serves? Is it not the one who reclines at the table? But I am among you as the one who serves'" (Luke 22:25-27).

God calls us to live with a heart of service toward others. To do this, we cannot be preoccupied with what we think we deserve or what people should be doing for us.

When we feel like our husband hasn't listened enough or our friends don't reach out enough or our kids don't help enough—we must remember that we will never give of ourselves more than what Christ has already given for us. We will never serve others more than He has served us.

For Additional Reflection: In what ways did Jesus demonstrate for us how to serve others? What can you do today to follow Jesus' example of serving and giving?

48. "As for me, I shall behold Your face in righteousness; I will be satisfied with Your likeness when I awake" (Psalm 17:15).

Before this verse, David describes people who only have their portion here on earth. This life is all they have. And so, any satisfaction they feel is only here with earthly things.

But in contrast, David knows that he will never be fully satisfied with the things here on earth. He knows that it is only when he sees Christ as He is and becomes like Him will he ever be satisfied.

I have often been easily distracted by the temporary satisfaction I might experience now, and looked toward so many things—relationships, acceptance, my home, and the list continues—to be my source of joy.

But whether people give us what we want or not, the truth is that the ultimate source of our fulfillment will be seeing and becoming like our Savior. As His attributes of humility, mercy, and lovingkindness grow in us, we become more like Him. This helps us serve others with the right perspective, which is living to please God and be like Him.

For additional reflection: How often do you think about being fully satisfied when you become like Jesus? Did you know that just hoping in Jesus actually has the power to make you more like Jesus now?

"Beloved, now we are children of God, and it has not appeared as yet what we will be. We know that <u>when He appears, we will be like Him</u>, because we will see Him just as He is. And <u>everyone who has this hope fixed on Him purifies himself</u>, just as He is pure" (1 John 3:2-3).

49. "Be kind to one another, tender-hearted, forgiving each other, just as God in Christ also has forgiven you" (Ephesians 4:32).

"Bearing with one another, and forgiving each other, whoever has a complaint against anyone; just as the Lord forgave you, so also should you" (Colossians 3:13).

In both of these verses, there is a "tit-for-tat," a "do it because" clause. Each time we are asked to forgive, we are reminded that we have first been forgiven by God. And the sins we've committed in offending God have been far worse than any sin committed against us.

It is always God's will for us to forgive, but we must understand what forgiveness is and isn't. Forgiveness is a choice to release the bitterness and anger you feel toward the person who hurt you. It is a choice to pray blessings for that person and pray for God to help that person.

But forgiveness is not a command to forget what has been done to you and put yourself in a foolish position so that it happens again. Forgiveness does not mean the sin was okay, but rather that because the offense was sin, it needs to be forgiven.

Forgiveness is not pardon. There may still be severe consequences for a person's sin. When God forgives, He also pardons. But our forgiveness is not God's forgiveness, and the person who sinned may still need to receive consequences—from us, if we are in a position of authority, or from the government, or from God.

But forgiveness does mean that we show love and kindness even to those who do not deserve it, because God has shown love and kindness first when we did not deserve it.

For additional reflection: Is there anyone in your life you may need to forgive today?

50. "Who are you to judge the servant of another? To his own master he stands or falls; and he will stand, for the Lord is able to make him stand...But you, why do you judge your brother? Or you again, why do you regard your brother with contempt? For we will all stand before the judgment seat of God...So then each one of us will give an account of himself to God. Therefore let us not judge one another anymore, but rather determine this— not to put an obstacle or a stumbling block in a brother's way" (Romans 14:4, 10, 12-13).

We often expect people to do certain things for us or play a certain role in our lives. We expect our lives to meet a certain standard or guarantee us certain things. But when those expectations we've placed on life and relationships go unmet, we often end up angry and disappointed.

For instance, someone might say, "I expected my husband to comfort me when I was feeling sad. He didn't, so now I feel angry with him for being so inconsiderate." We see our husband's failure, but we fail to see the huge part we play in our own hurt feelings because of the expectation we placed on our husband.

Instead of placing conditions on our love for others, we must remember that each person will give an account to God. Our role is not to treat others based on how they deserve to be treated, but on how God commands us to treat them.

For additional reflection: Have you expected things from others—a spouse, a child, a leader, a pastor, a friend, a parent—and their failure to meet your expectations caused you to live with judgment, harshness, and/or unforgiveness toward them? Is it okay to withhold kindness, love or honor from someone because they don't meet your personal expectations? What will you do today so that you show grace, forgiveness, and love to others?

Reflections 51–60 ~ Believing God's

Grace is Sufficient

51. "Because of the surpassing greatness of the revelations, for this reason, to keep me from exalting myself, there was given me a thorn in the flesh, a messenger of Satan to torment me—to keep me from exalting myself! Concerning this I implored the Lord three times that it might leave me. And He has said to me, '<u>My grace is sufficient for you, for power is perfected in weakness</u>.' Most gladly, therefore, I will rather boast about my weaknesses, so that the power of Christ may dwell in me. Therefore I am well content with weaknesses, with insults, with distresses, with persecutions, with difficulties, for Christ's sake; for when I am weak, then I am strong" (2 Corinthians 12:7-10).

Think with me for a minute about Paul's remarkable life. After being stopped by God on the Damascus road and becoming a Christian, God used him powerfully as the apostle to the Gentiles.

Paul planted churches, wrote letters that would become books of the New Testament, and experienced heaven so intimately that he didn't know if he was in his body or out of his body.

And while Paul was persecuted greatly, his experiences with God—the CREATOR of all things—might have still inclined him to be prideful. So God allowed a messenger of Satan to *torment* him.

Now Paul was close to God, and he pleaded with God three times to remove the "thorn" that tormented him. And though God could have removed the thorn, instead He reminded Paul that His grace would be sufficient. That's it. God said, "My grace is sufficient for you, for power is perfected in weakness."

And often, the thorns in our life are not removed so God can teach us the same truth He taught Paul—that His grace is enough. Knowing that having God's grace during suffering is sufficient, even when the suffering continues, have you ever wondered what it means tangibly to "have God's grace"?

God's grace is sufficient for us—it is all we need. And when we go to God's throne of grace, He gives us mercy and grace for our time of need. But how does this "grace" sustain us? How does it help us? Paul's thorn wasn't removed, which mean he still suffered. What does having grace look like when we are suffering?

Additionally, when God isn't answering our prayers, how exactly do we know we have His grace? We would think that His grace would be most evident by *giving us what we want right when we want it.*

When God immediately and obviously answers a prayer request, my thought is, "Wow, God has been so gracious to me. Praise God."

But when those prayers are not answered, my first thought is not always, "Wow, God has been so gracious to me. Praise God." Rather, I don't always feel like God's grace is enough because I don't always feel like I have His grace.

So back to my prior question, What does it mean tangibly to have God's grace? And how can we have God's grace in such a way that we can say with Paul, "God's grace is sufficient for me."?

Here is why God's grace is sufficient. What we have in Christ is of far greater value, far more precious, far more satisfying that whatever we may want on earth.

Think of what it means to have God's grace as a child of God and co-heir with Christ. We see God's lavish grace toward us when God chose us before the foundation of the world so He could forgive us, give us His righteousness, make us like Jesus, deliver us from judgment, and cause us to live with Him in full satisfaction forever.

Let me make a comparison for you. Imagine wanting a tent and being told, "The mansion I've given you with the five car garage, the built in pool, the landscaped acreage, the exclusive neighborhood, the underground bowling alley, the fully stocked chef's kitchen, the gorgeous furniture, and the breathtaking view—these are sufficient for you. You can be content with the mansion even if you don't receive a tent."

I over-described the mansion to emphasize how lavish and extravagant God's grace is compared to the thing we may want and not have.

When we obsess over what's not right—when we focus so hard on that thing we need or want or the problem we want fixed or that marriage issue or that financial situation—when we obsess about the things we want so much that our focus and hope becomes placed on that instead of the grace to be brought, we set ourselves up for continual disappointment, grief, anxiety, bitterness and self-pity.

So back when I would feel like I didn't have God's grace, my feelings were seriously misleading. God's grace is never half-hearted or partial. His grace is always lavish and abundant. His grace toward me in all that He has already done for me and all that He is going to do is enough, even if I don't have everything I want. His grace is enough.

For additional reflection: Have you ever felt that maybe God didn't answer a prayer because He was stuck or limited by some earthly event or person? When God did not answer Paul's prayer, what did God want Paul to understand? *It was more important for Paul to understand <u>God's grace is sufficient</u> than for God to grant his request.*

In what ways are the things we want here on earth like "tents" compared to all we will receive in heaven?

52. "But God, being rich in mercy, because of His great love with which He loved us, even when we were dead in our transgressions, made us alive together with Christ (<u>by grace you have been saved</u>)" (Ephesians 2:5).

"For <u>by grace you have been saved</u> through faith; and that not of yourselves, <u>it is the gift of God</u>" (Ephesians 2:8).

"Being <u>justified as a gift by His grace</u> through the redemption which is in Christ Jesus" (Romans 3:24).

Grace from God is unmerited favor, undeserved kindness. Our salvation is a gift from God, a result of His grace. Just

125

as a dead person cannot bring themselves to life, when we were spiritually dead in sins, God made us alive. He forgives us of all our sin and declares us righteous in Christ.

All of this is His *gift*. We are given salvation because of His grace. We are awaiting glory because of His grace. Every good thing we have in this life is a result of His grace.

For additional reflection: What are some additional benefits that result from our salvation according to the following verses?

"And these whom He predestined, He also called; and these whom He called, He also justified; and these whom He justified, He also glorified" (Romans 8:30).

"After you have suffered for a little while, the God of all grace, who called you to His eternal glory in Christ, will Himself perfect, confirm, strengthen and establish you" (1Peter 5:10).

53. "Therefore let us draw near with confidence to the throne of grace, so that we may receive mercy and find grace to help in time of need" (Hebrews 4:16).

Every day I desperately need God's grace to abound toward me. Every day there are "thorns" in my life, and those thorns give me an opportunity to choose whether I will feel sorry for myself and get angry at the problems, or learn by experience that His grace is sufficient for me.

We may find ourselves in circumstances where we are unhappy with what is happening. But we can't let those disappointing circumstances keep us from recognizing the grace that has been given to us in Christ. We can't let circumstances determine whether or not we will be content with what we have.

Did you notice that God answered Paul's prayer and yet Paul's circumstances didn't change? God answered the prayer by telling Paul that His grace was sufficient.

This is what contentment looks like. This is what trusting God looks like. It means being content with God's presence and His grace.

127

For additional reflection: Think about asking the Lord for something three times—something that means a lot to you—and instead of getting your request, you receive the answer, "My grace is sufficient for you." What would it look like in your life to fully believe that God's grace is enough?

54. "After calling the apostles in, they flogged them and ordered them not to speak in the name of Jesus, and then released them. So they went on their way from the presence of the Council, rejoicing that they had been considered worthy to suffer shame for His name" (Acts 5:40-41).

Many times we feel sorry for ourselves because we don't have the things we most want. We feel sorry for ourselves for the situation we are in instead of thanking God in the midst of that situation. We feel angry or upset instead of rejoicing at the opportunity to suffer for Christ.

Just because circumstances are bad is not a reflection of what God has for you. What God has for you is ultimately going to be seen in eternity. What happens is often we suffer with Him now because we are going to be glorified together with Him.

Knowing that we will be glorified with Him, we can be content, even when our house isn't the size we wish it was, or we don't make that meeting we really wanted to be at, or we didn't get that promotion or we didn't get that husband, or we didn't have those children or we didn't have this or that or all the things we think we need. And that doesn't mean God is not going to give it to us in this life, but while we wait we can be content because our ultimate glory is going to be revealed with Jesus in eternity.

And God does bless us while we are here on earth. His joy, Himself, His Word, His comfort even now in this life. He often blesses us even beyond that by giving us families, food, children, homes, clothes and sometimes even good food and cute clothes and other blessings.

For additional reflection: How is God's grace toward us through our salvation and the blessings that follow—

including eternal life—enough even if we don't immediately receive what we want here on earth?

55. "I will ask the Father, and He will give you another Helper, that He may be with you forever; that is the Spirit of truth, whom the world cannot receive, because it does not see Him or know Him, but you know Him because He abides with you and will be in you" (John 14:16-17).

When Jesus returned to the Father, He sent the Holy Spirit to the believers as a helper and comforter on the day of Pentecost. And to this day, everyone who believes in Jesus receives the Spirit of truth, God's Holy Spirit, and we are sealed as a guarantee of our inheritance. (Ephesians 1:13-14)

"Now may the God of hope fill you with all joy and peace in believing, so that <u>you will abound in hope by the power of the Holy Spirit</u>" (Romans 15:13).

Because we know the Holy Spirit lives in us, we need to say "God has made me able to do the things He calls me to do. His Spirit is alive and powerful and dwells in me."

For additional reflection: "But I say, walk by the Spirit, and you will not carry out the desire of the flesh...But if you are led by the Spirit, you are not under the Law...Now those who belong to Christ Jesus have crucified the flesh with its passions and desires. If we live by the Spirit, let us also walk by the Spirit" (Galatians 5:16,18,24-25).

The Holy Spirit gives us the power to do what pleases God. Because we now have the power of the Holy Spirit, we don't need a law because the Spirit causes us to do what is right.

How does this amazing truth give us hope that no sin or struggle will be too hard to overcome?

56. "For this finds favor, if for the sake of conscience toward God a person bears up under sorrows when

suffering unjustly. For what credit is there if, when you sin and are harshly treated, you endure it with patience? But if when you do what is right and suffer for it you patiently endure it, this finds favor with God. For you have been called for this purpose, since Christ also suffered for you, leaving you an example for you to follow in His steps WHO COMMITTED NO SIN, NOR WAS ANY DECEIT FOUND IN HIS MOUTH; and while being reviled, He did not revile in return; while suffering, He uttered no threats, but kept entrusting Himself to Him who judges righteously" (1 Peter 2:19-23).

We can easily trick ourselves into believing that Jesus feels sorry for us. That because He cares for us, He must share our frustration toward those people who let us down. And since He grieves with us, we are not sure why He won't deliver us. When in reality, Jesus is the one who came to serve, who even came to suffer, who "gave us an example that we should follow His steps."

For additional reflection: What is a verse you could meditate on when difficult times come? Is there a verse you have meditated on in the past during difficult times?

What do you love about these verses? What from these verses brings you comfort?

57. "Make sure that your character is free from the love of money, being content with what you have; for He Himself has said, 'I WILL NEVER DESERT YOU, NOR WILL I EVER FORSAKE YOU'" (Hebrews 13:5).

Be content with what you have, because God will never leave you or forsake you. The truth is, God is enough. His grace is enough. Because He will never leave, we have all we need.

For additional reflection: How does not being content with what we have show that we doubt God is enough?

Fill in the blanks in the following sentence. "I feel sorry for myself because _____ and I would be happy if only I had _____, but God's grace is sufficient for me because God will *never* leave me and He will *never* forsake me. And that is enough. It is better than everything else I may want or need."

58. "Worthy are You, our Lord and our God, to receive glory and honor and power; for You created all things, and because of Your will they existed, and were created" (Revelation 4:11).

"Set your mind on the things above, not on the things that are on earth. For you have died and your life is hidden with Christ in God" (Colossians 3:2-3).

Self-pity says that what is "wrong" in our life is more worthy of our thoughts and our focus than God is of our trust and gratitude.

When we set our minds on the things we are unhappy with—the faults of our husband, the size of our house, the issues with our friends or parents, our weight or how we look, or any one of a million other things—we become even more unhappy and discontent.

But in Christ, I've died. My selfish ambition, my worldly desires, my vain hopes, those died with me. I died when I chose to follow Christ and be crucified with Him. "I have been crucified with Christ; and it is no longer I who live, but Christ lives in me; and the life which I now live in the flesh I live by faith in the Son of God, who loved me and gave Himself up for me" (Galatians 2:20).

Does this mean those worldly desires and selfish ambitions will never be seen again? No, they will still call me and pull me and try to keep me sidetracked from what matters in life. But I have to remind myself that I'm dead and my life is no longer about me.

And because I'm dead, what does it matter how I'm treated? Katie is dead. They are treating Christ this way. When I recognize that I'm dead, that my life is gone and hidden in Christ, then I'm done self-seeking, living in a way that my life becomes about beauty, fame, popularity, the best house, whatever.

My life is now about what Christ calls me to be about and only what He calls me to be about. Did He call me to be a mother? Then I will pour my heart into training my children to love and follow God. Did He call me to be a wife? Then I will serve and love my husband selflessly, as an ambassador of Christ. Did He call me to serve in the Children's Ministry at church? Then I will do my best every week to teach those children as well as I can so they will understand God's Word and understand His love for them. Did He call me to suffer? Then I will suffer humbly and willingly for His glory, because I belong fully to Him.

And whatever He calls me to do, I will work my hardest and keep learning His Word so I can live pleasing to Him, so I will better understand what He says about His desires for me and not what I assume He might want.

When I forget that I've been crucified with Christ, my life becomes about me. Instead of living for Jesus, I live for Katie. I see it in the way I respond to people. I see it in the things that fight for my attention.

Instead of devotion that says, "Lord, take anything, everything, whatever you want. It's yours because I've died. My life is gone now, hidden in You." I hold on to what is mine and mistrust God's goodness. When I remember that I've been crucified with Christ, then I desire to know God more, to obey Him fully, and to honor Him completely.

For additional reflection: What has God called you to do in your life? How can you fulfill that role as one who has died and whose life is hidden with Christ?

59. "And the grace of our Lord was more than abundant, with the faith and love which are found in Christ Jesus" (1 Timothy 1:14).

When we *don't* believe God's grace is enough, we believe that we know better than God. When we *do* believe God's grace is enough, then even in the face of unanswered prayers or continued suffering, if God gives us His grace, we believe it is an adequate answer.

One of the primary differences between the prosperity gospel and the true gospel is not whether or not God will make us rich, happy, and free from sickness or disease, but *when*. The prosperity gospel teaches that God will do

137

it as soon as you have enough faith to make it happen. The Bible teaches God will do it as soon as you are made like Christ and inherit all things with Him.

Now, God gives wealth and happiness and health and long life here on earth as it pleases Him according to His will, according to far more details than we are able to know. But all of us who are born of God will become joint heirs with Christ, and every promise we might want here on earth and so many more will be ours in eternity forever.

For additional reflection: "And God is able to make all grace abound to you, so that always having all sufficiency in everything, you may have an abundance for every good deed" (2 Corinthians 9:8).

The NIV version helps bring clarity to verse above: "And God is able to bless you abundantly, so that in all things at all times, having all that you need, you will abound in every good work" (2 Corinthians 9:8 NIV).

Using this verse as a guide, answer the following questions:

How much grace is God able to make abound toward you? For what things does God give this grace? How often can you have this grace? How much of this grace do you get for every good work?

60. "But as for me, my feet came close to stumbling, my steps had almost slipped. For I was envious of the arrogant as I saw the prosperity of the wicked…Behold, these are the wicked; and always at ease, they have increased in wealth…When I pondered to understand this, it was troublesome in my sight until I came into the sanctuary of God; then I perceived their end… Nevertheless I am continually with You; You have taken hold of my right hand. With Your counsel You will guide me, and afterward receive me to glory. Whom have I in heaven but You? And besides You, I desire nothing on earth. My flesh and my heart may fail, but God is the strength of my heart and my portion forever" (Psalm 73:2-3,12,16-17,23-26).

While it may seem as though wicked people prosper unfairly, the Psalmist was able to accept this when he remembered how it will end for them. "Surely You set them in slippery places; You cast them down to destruction. How they are destroyed in a moment! They are utterly swept away by sudden terrors!" (Psalm 73:18-19).

While their end is destruction, we will be received to glory! These verses from Psalm 73 have impacted me many times when I wanted something so much that it consumed my thoughts.

I remember when I was still single and had a crush on a guy. During the time when I became consumed with the crush, I read these verses, and it was as if the Lord reminded me, "I'm over here." And then I ran back into God's grace, remembering He is the One who will always be faithful, who will always love me, who will always care.

The things I want will come and go, but God will be my God forever. That's why I can say with the Psalmist, "And besides You, I desire nothing on earth." It's my relationship with God that is my most precious relationship. He is the ultimate love of my life, my sufficiency, a far greater treasure than anything the wicked will ever possess.

For additional reflection: Have you ever expended more strength wanting (or striving for) what God can give than you gave to loving God?

Dear Lord, please cause me to want you more than everything else, to <u>believe</u> and rejoice that your grace is enough. Help me to remember that You take hold of my right hand and You will receive me to glory. Help me to treasure my relationship with You more than anything else I may want in this life.

Reflections 61–70 ~ Victory in Trusting God

61. "No temptation has overtaken you but such as is common to man; and God is faithful, who will not allow you to be tempted beyond what you are able, but with the temptation will provide the way of escape also, so that you will be able to endure it" (1 Corinthians 10:13).

As long as we keep telling ourselves that we can't put up with much more, that we can't deal with these problems any longer, then we will live defeated.

We need to say "I will keep pressing on because of this high calling from God. He is for me. He is my helper. He is my strength. He has made me able to do this."

"Not that I have already obtained it or have already become perfect, but I press on so that I may lay hold of that for which also I was laid hold of by Christ Jesus'" (Philippians 3:12).

For additional reflection: Fill in the blanks. Though I may be tempted to feel _____, I know that God will give me His grace to escape the temptation. When I feel tempted, I will believe that God has made me able to resist sin and I will run to Him for help.

62. "But the salvation of the righteous is from the LORD; He is their strength in time of trouble" (Psalm 37:39).

"For I am confident of this very thing, that He who began a good work in you will perfect it until the day of Christ Jesus" (Philippians 1:6).

As long as you desire God and want to honor Him, even though you may not have the time or resources or opportunities or abilities to serve Him like you wish you could, He is still doing a perfect work in your life, and you will still be presented perfect on the day of Christ Jesus.

But until that day, it often feels like we are waiting on God. Maybe you want God to move faster—to let you serve Him in a bigger capacity—and you'd prefer it if He hurried. Even the Psalmist prayed that God would not delay. (Psalm 40:17; 70:5)

Often we believe God is powerful enough but we wonder why He moves so slow, why our prayers take so long to be answered, and why we are not better equipped or more resourced or talented for what He may have called us to do. We doubt that God's timing is perfect and almost doubt if He is able to move faster. (Like He would if He could but we're not sure He can.) We struggle to believe everything is where He wants it.

But here is the thing, the *tension* is at the perfect level. Your life may not be perfect, but the tension in your life is. I don't mean anxiety, but rather that place where we are waiting on God but wrestling with His silence. The place where there is a pull on our hearts and we must *trust* Him because the answer has not come.

All through the Bible—David and his Psalms, Abraham and His journeys, Moses and the Israelites—God's people were constantly in that place of pressure, of having to call out to God and *wait* on Him.

You see, God's delay in resolving our trouble—that what we view as taking too long—is actually part of a plan far better than we currently see.

For additional reflection: "But as for me, I trust in You, O LORD, I say, 'You are my God.' My times are in Your hand" (Psalm 31:14-15a).

If your times are in God's hand, meaning that Your life is on schedule with His timeline, what does that mean about God's "delays" and unanswered prayer?

63. "For it is God who is at work in you, both to will and to work for His good pleasure" (Philippians 2:13).

"Now the God of peace, who brought up from the dead the great Shepherd of the sheep through the blood of the eternal covenant, even Jesus our Lord, equip you in every good thing to do His will, working in us that which is pleasing in His sight, through Jesus Christ, to whom be the glory forever and ever. Amen" (Hebrews 13:20-21).

Not only is God working in your life and directing your steps, but He is working in you. Jesus is growing and perfecting your faith.

The outcome of our faith is the salvation of our souls. We often forget that our stay here on earth is only for a brief time. But when things are hard, we feel like they will last forever. They won't. God has promised us an inheritance that will never perish, and right now it is being reserved for us.

We will be in heaven before we know it and all these trials will never be part of our lives again. So we live for today, but with a vision of forever.

God loves you eternally. He will work everything in your life together for good after the counsel of His will. It will be wonderful in the end. When eternity comes, you will never regret saying, "Not my will, Lord, but yours be done."

Our hope is great because it is eternal. We don't obey Christ and then perish forever. Paul says, "If we have hoped in Christ in this life only, we are of all men most to be pitied" (1 Corinthians 15:19). If we obey God and then die to never rise again, even Paul admits that our lives would be the most miserable of all people.

Rather, our obedience, our sacrifice to do what glorifies God, is working for us an eternal reward. We are investing in our eternal relationship with Christ. We rejoice with inexpressible joy because we love God and believe in Him, while we look forward to *the end of our faith, the salvation of our souls.* (1 Peter 1:8-9)

For additional reflection: "In this you greatly rejoice, even though now for a little while, if necessary, you have been distressed by various trials, so that the proof of your faith, being more precious than gold which is perishable, even though tested by fire, may be found to result in praise and glory and honor at the revelation of Jesus Christ" (1 Peter 1:6-7).

According to the verse above, during this time on earth we may be distressed by various trials, but what is being tested in those trials? What is the result of this testing?

64. "We destroy arguments and every lofty opinion raised against the knowledge of God, and take every thought captive to obey Christ" (2 Corinthians 10:5 ESV).

When we think in such a way that we sin with our thoughts—complaining, bitterness, unthankfulness—then those thoughts are exalting themselves over the knowledge of God.

Ask God to cause His Spirit to govern your thoughts, because "the mind set on the Spirit is life and peace." (Romans 8:6)

For additional reflection: Our thoughts can determine how we feel. When we think in a way that pleases Christ, there is life and peace. What strategies can you use to keep your mind set on the Spirit?

65. "I am the LORD your God...You shall have no other gods before Me" (Exodus 20:2a,3).

God wants us to love Him with ALL our strength, to love Him more than we love what He can give.

When we love something so much that it keeps us from fully loving God, that something can be called an idol. And the Bible has a lot to say about idols. In the Old Testament, many people worshipped statues they could make with their hands and see with their eyes.

Many of the idols we worship today are not statues we keep in our homes, but they are anything we desire more than God. These desires could also be called "gods."

God begins the Ten Commandments by saying, "I am the LORD your God...You shall have no other gods before Me" (Exodus 20:2a,3). I used to read this command and believe I had never broken it. But later I understood that we make a god of anything we love, worship, serve, desire, honor, fear, enjoy, or depend on more than God.

In the New Testament, the Greek gods Artemis, Zeus, and Hermes are mentioned in the book of Acts because their names are part of the stories from Paul's missionary journeys. (Acts 14:11-18; 19:23-41)

Artemis was considered the god of animals, hunting, childbirth, the protector of young girls, and disease in women. Zeus was considered the god of thunder and the sky. Hermes was considered a protector of travelers.

When I thought about the worship and love people gave to these gods, it struck me that the people didn't likely *love* Artemis, Zeus, Hermes, or any of the other gods. Rather, they loved the <u>benefits</u> they believed they would get by worshiping these gods.

If they worshipped Artemis, they believed Artemis would protect their young girls and heal their sick women. If they worshipped Zeus, the weather would be favorable. Hermes would protect them. Their worship of these gods was a means to get what they wanted.

And as a human race, we still love money, health, fertility, safety, and favorable weather (especially if we don't have air conditioning or heating to endure bad weather). While we may not use the "names" of gods to refer to what we want, we still seek the same benefits the ancient Greeks sought.

And so our love of what we want can keep us from wholeheartedly loving God. Mark 12:30 says, "AND YOU SHALL LOVE THE LORD YOUR GOD WITH ALL YOUR HEART, AND WITH ALL YOUR SOUL, AND WITH ALL YOUR MIND, AND WITH ALL YOUR STRENGTH."

The danger in not loving God with all our heart, soul, strength, and mind is that we are tempted to worship and long for other things more than we worship and long for God. Instead of expending our effort to love God fully, our effort is given to longing for His gifts. Our love for God must consume us. It must be our greatest passion in life.

Until we determine to make loving God our greatest desire, we will never be fully free of self-pity. As long as we desire other things more than God, we will never experience the untroubled heart that results from trusting Him.

We have the choice to seek God and cry out for a deeper relationship with Him or to cry out for a million other things. The more we love God above all other things, the more victory we will gain in trusting Him.

For additional reflection: What "gods" have you been tempted to "worship"? In other words, what benefits— money, health, good relationships, children, ministry, career, husband, etc.—have you been tempted to desire more than Christ? Why do you think Jesus said, "No one can serve two masters; for either he will hate the one and love the other, or he will be devoted to one and despise the other. You cannot serve God and wealth" (Matthew 6:24)?

66. "Humble yourselves in the presence of the Lord, and He will exalt you" (James 4:10).

"Therefore humble yourselves under the mighty hand of God, that He may exalt you at the proper time" (1 Peter 5:6).

"For thus says the high and exalted One Who lives forever, whose name is Holy, 'I dwell on a high and holy place, and also with the contrite and lowly of spirit In order to revive the spirit of the lowly and to revive the heart of the contrite" (Isaiah 57:15).

Maybe what you are suffering is meant to increase your humility so that you will abundantly glorify God when His answer comes. Humility is the prerequisite for honor. God values humility so much that He requires it in the person He exalts, in the person He revives, and in the person who draws near to Him.

If pain and difficulty is necessary to increase our humility, it will all be worth it in the end. Because humility is a requirement for closeness with Jesus, it is worth any price to gain humility.

For additional reflection: Have you seen how specific types of suffering have caused your humility, compassion for others, and dependence on God to increase?

Why do you think humility is so necessary to God?

67. "I know how to get along with humble means, and I also know how to live in prosperity; in any and every circumstance I have learned the secret of being filled and going hungry, both of having abundance and suffering need. I can do all things through Him who strengthens me" (Philippians 4:12-13).

One snare of not trusting God is feeling helpless. Instead of feeling capable of contentment, knowing Christ gives us the strength we need, we feel powerless to cope with the situation we're in and powerless to bear up under the problems we face.

Instead, we need to say "I know God is good, even though life is hard. And I know God's grace is sufficient for me. God is enough. Because I have God, I have all I need. Because I know God can do all things, I also know He is able to make a weak, sin-prone person such as myself able to be content in all circumstances."

For additional reflection: How can difficult times strengthen your relationship with Jesus and draw you closer to Him?

68. "Come to Me, all who are weary and heavy-laden, and I will give you rest. Take My yoke upon you and learn from Me, for I am gentle and humble in heart, and YOU WILL FIND REST FOR YOUR SOULS. For My yoke is easy and My burden is light" (Matthew 11:28-30).

His yoke is easy when we *trust* Him. When the issue that weighs you down today—the one you've prayed to be fixed and it's not, the one that makes you feel stuck in a hopeless situation—presses against your heart, remember that that pressure is meant to be there. Like braces which pull the teeth where they need to go, so the pressure pulls our character where it needs to go.

Maybe you say, "I know I'm not perfect but I also don't have any serious sin that God needs to deal with." I'm reminded that Jesus was perfect, that His character was *perfect*, and yet "He learned obedience from the things which He suffered" (Hebrews 5:8). When much is asked of us, we learn to obey in a far greater capacity.

If it was up to me, all my prayers would be answered and as a result, I wouldn't experience suffering. There would be no stressful situations, no unanswered prayers, no painful impasses. God would instantly answer every prayer but I would never learn to deeply obey or deeply trust. The depth of character that comes from obeying God in the hardest times would be lacking in me. And I would miss out on the intimacy of knowing Christ through fellowship with His sufferings. (Philippians 3:10)

Knowing that Jesus offers rest—and the trials we face are not restful—then we must learn how to rest in the midst of the trials. We must learn to *rest in Him* in the places of greatest pressure. This is a result of trusting Him, of believing that He has us in His hand and He loves us beyond our comprehension.

For additional reflection: Psalm 56:8-9 says, "You have taken account of my wanderings; Put my tears in Your bottle. Are they not in Your book? Then my enemies will turn back in the day when I call; This I know, that God is for me."

What does this verse say that God does with your tears. Do you believe that God is for you (on your side)?

69. "The Spirit Himself testifies with our spirit that we are children of God, and <u>if children, heirs also, heirs of God and fellow heirs with Christ</u>, if indeed we suffer with Him so that we may also be glorified with Him" (Romans 8:16-17).

We are fellow heirs with Christ! We are sharing an inheritance with Jesus!

Imagine knowing that you were going to be splitting an inheritance with the only son of a billionaire. How would you feel about being chosen to receive such a great gift? And yet we have been chosen to receive something far greater.

So what is this inheritance we will share with Jesus? "In these last days [God] has spoken to us in <u>His Son, whom He appointed heir of all things</u>, through whom also He made the world" (Hebrews 1:2).

Jesus is the heir of all things! So not only are we joint heirs with Jesus, but He is going to inherit everything.

What does it mean to inherit all things? It means you're getting everything. There is nothing you won't have. When the day comes and Christ receives His inheritance, you will also receive it. Everything means this whole earth and everything on it. Every acre of land. Every mile of the shoreline. Every star and galaxy in space. Christ will reign and we will reign with Him.

"So then let no one boast in men. <u>For all things belong to you</u>, whether Paul or Apollos or Cephas or the world or life or death or things present or things to come; <u>all things belong to you</u>, and you belong to Christ; and Christ belongs to God" (1 Corinthians 3:21-23).

If you are the co-heir of the son of a billionaire, and that billionaire died yesterday, your financial circumstances are good even though you are still waiting for the money to be distributed.

While you may have little here on earth, you are a joint heir with Christ, and He is the heir of all things, so all things are yours. The things you lack now are only temporary, but what you gain as an heir of Christ will be eternal.

For additional reflection: Based on the verses in this reflection, what is your hope in eternity?

70. "We have obtained an inheritance, having been predestined according to His purpose <u>who works all things after the counsel of His will</u>" (Ephesians 1:11).

When we let discouraging thoughts influence our minds, our vision is short-sighted. "I am never going to be free from this situation. I will never be good enough for this thing I want to do. I will never have this thing I want."

When we trust God, we live victoriously. "If the Lord wills, I will be free from this situation. I will have this thing I want. I will be exactly who and where God wants me to be."

Maybe God wants to show you that you cannot do this thing you want or have this thing you want on your own so that when the time comes and He gives you your heart's desire, you will know without a doubt that God made it happen. And instead of taking this gift for granted, you will abound with gratitude.

Maybe the time is near for you to see God's answer, to receive His deliverance, and to have your desire fulfilled. But maybe God wants your heart to be ready, to be empty so He can fill it, and to be reliant on Him so He can be glorified. And maybe He has allowed this season of suffering and difficulty because it was the greatest way, the most glorious path, to the coming results.

I pray God will give you the desire of your heart and answer the prayers you have asked.

"May he give you the desire of your heart and make all your plans succeed" (Psalm 20:4 NIV).

But additionally, I pray that whether you see God's answer in this life or not, you would trust God with thankfulness and praise whatever the outcome. I pray you would always remember God loves you deeply and eternally and nothing can ever separate you from His love. And I pray your heart would echo the words of Jesus in saying, "Abba! Father! <u>All things are possible for You</u>; remove this cup from Me; <u>yet not what I will, but what You will</u>" (Mark 14:36).

"For I am convinced that neither death, nor life, nor angels, nor principalities, nor things present, nor things to come, nor powers, nor height, nor depth, nor any other created thing, will be able to separate us from the love of God, which is in Christ Jesus our Lord" (Romans 8:38-39).

For additional reflection: In what ways might God be using the trials in your life, the things you are waiting for, and the regrets you have to prepare you for what God has in your future?

Epilogue: How to be Content With Your Calling

Sometimes when we are in the heat of a trial, we aren't thinking much of our calling or any ministry, but simply hoping to make it through. But when the burdens lift, we may find ourselves feeling a bit lost. We may wonder what we offer the world, or we might feel that we've missed out on accomplishing anything great.

I've felt so often that if I'm really serving God, I'll have a huge ministry, a successful Bible study series, a multitude of converts, SOMETHING BIG to show for it. That everyone will notice how radically I live for Jesus.

But the reality is that I don't stand out and my day to day life is far more about cleaning and dishes and homeschooling and paying bills and potty training than it is about remarkable missionary work in some foreign country.

And so I've felt like a bit of a Christian failure. The "mundane" things that my life consists of will probably never make it into the next printing of "Trial and Triumph" or any of the other biographies of great Christians.

At some point in our Christian life, most of us create standards of "godliness." We take what we know about God and His Word and then we define what are lives will look like if we are "godly." Or maybe we use another word—"fully devoted" "on fire" "radical" "committed believer" and on the list goes.

What does a godly woman look like to you? Is her life filled with great accomplishments, daring missionary work, and world changing evangelism? Does she talk about Jesus with everyone she meets? Does she leave gospel tracts at the gas station? Is she well known for her good works? Do people tell stories of her godly acts? Is her house spotless and her laundry always done? Do her children always obey? Does she show up on time every week to church? What do you believe defines godliness?

And what does this all matter? If you've ever strived to be a godly woman, you know this struggle. If you've ever pursued God but hoped people would say "she's been with Jesus," you know what I'm talking about.

I know that a godly woman fears the Lord. But how we define the "works" that accompany fearing the Lord differ. Some people might think the godliest woman is the one who passes out the most gospel tracts, or the one who leads worship with the most emotion, or the one who teaches in the most life-impacting way.

I had certain ideas of what a godly woman would look like in my mind for so long—ideas that drove my everyday actions, my goals, and my disappointment when I did not meet that standard of godliness—that when I began to seriously search the Scripture for myself about how a godly *woman* lives, it was shocking to me.

Now I understood a wife is to reverence her husband and love her children and those things. But what I thought for so long was that a woman's walk with God should pretty much look almost the same as a man's walk with God, minus the pastoring part.

If God sent out seventy-two disciples to preach the gospel, surely He wanted me to always be preaching the gospel. If God sent Paul on radical missionary journeys, surely God would want me to go on radical missionary journeys. If Ezekiel was given the instruction to warn the people about God's coming judgment, surely it must be my calling to also warn people about God's coming judgment. And as I read about every *man* in Scripture whom God called for a life of witnessing and missionary work, I assumed that it was just a coincidence that only men were usually mentioned.

But as I began to really evaluate what God wanted me to do to serve Him, I thought through the great things that each person in Biblical history did, and I was stuck by several things.

1.   Most of the great "action" items were accomplished by men. Preaching the gospel and evangelism (Pentecost, the seventy-two sent out by Jesus, Paul preaching in the temple each Sabbath), healing the sick, doing miracles, interpreting dreams, leading the Israelites, planting churches—all involved men.

2.   There are a lot of famous men who didn't do great "action" things and yet they still led great lives. Abraham—his great work was simply believing God (and God counted it to him as righteousness). Job—he did not curse God during difficulty. Shadrach, Meshach, and Abednego—they did not go out looking to preach to the

king, but God brought the king to them when they simply would not worship anyone but God.

3.   The great things most of the women did were things we can relate to. Timothy's mother and grandmother trained him to understand the Scriptures. Dorcas made clothing for others. Sarah obeyed her husband. Lydia opened her home for church meetings. Ruth supported her mother-in-law and worshipped the true God. Great lives lived by doing the required things well.

I want to go back to Abraham. Remember, Abraham's great work was just believing God. At the moment when Abraham believed God and it was counted to him as righteousness, did fireworks pop in the sky? Did people clap? Did he become instantly famous and admired for the one thing that changed history forever? Did his act of faith become instantly known throughout the world? No, it was between him and the Lord. God saw. But that was everything. And it was enough.

Job's great work was continuing to bless God during difficulty. Yet we often overlook the value of these simple things in our own lives. But maybe they are most precious thing we do. Maybe we have undervalued *simple obedience*: Training our children to follow God. Obeying and loving our husbands when it's hardest. Believing God for salvation. Trusting God when life is falling apart. Providing hospitality and generosity to others. Maybe in our search for godliness, we've forgotten that these *are* the great things? That these are what make a life great? That these things are what make your life count for eternity?

Maybe while we are looking for a life that seems more significant, more impacting, more powerful, we are already standing in the place that God has ordained for us? That we are not missing out like we so often think, but if we are living to please God, we have no lack. We have not fallen short of godliness, but maybe that what seems mundane is really glorious?

Now if you are a missionary in a foreign country or you love evangelism, I'm so blessed that you are part of the same body of Christ as I. You are awesome. And maybe you are in a different season of life than I am. While some women may have the freedom to go street witnessing, others are wise to consider the safety of their young children.

But it's easy to compare myself to women with no kids or those whose kids have grown—or to men—who are even more different than my life and calling. It's easy to compare myself with Billy Graham or Paul the Apostle when Tabitha from the New Testament is a far more realistic role model. Her valuable contribution to the church was not evangelism or missions or teaching or worship but rather it was sewing. She generously made and distributed garments to her church family. And she is remembered as "abounding with deeds of kindness and charity." (Acts 9:36)

I decided to think through the biblical examples of women we are given—and not just every woman in the Bible—but specifically those who are *praised*. Those women who are not only mentioned but who are called virtuous or who are praised or those whom we are told to follow.

- Dorcas—praised for her good works, which was sewing garments for the believers.

- Proverbs 31 Woman—praised for being virtuous because of her wisdom with earning and

168

investing money, her diligence, and her fear of the Lord.

- Sarah—praised for honoring and obeying her husband when her comfort and well-being were at risk.

- Ruth—praised for being virtuous because she devoted her life to her grief-stricken mother-in-law.

Each of these women were praised for doing the things that we also have opportunities to do. And in remembering these women, I felt so much comfort in knowing that we don't have to be doing "great things" for God to be wholeheartedly serving Him.

By focusing on how I am not standing out in my radical life of obedience, I was actually becoming discontent with the place God has me. I want to be discontent with every area of my life that is not like Christ, but content with everything I do that is pleasing to God—no matter how insignificant or unrecognized that is.

I equated great things with making my life really count for eternity. I saw doing important things as more important to God than contentment for the small place I was in. I was not happy to live in the day of small things.

The life we have likely doesn't seem "great." Our daily lives don't seem remarkable. We are not standing before thousands preaching the gospel like Peter or married to a king and pleading for the lives of our people like Esther. But maybe it is in this smallness that God is doing something great.

When we feel like we are not as "godly" as the imaginary standard we've created in our mind, we can remember these things:

1. Our contentment with whatever calling God gives us is better than our discontentment with a calling He has not given us.

2. We can vitally support any person we want in the world simply by praying for them. PRAY PRAY PRAY. We can be a support role in ANYONE'S life through prayer, whether we get to interact with them or not. The president, the government, pastors, our children, our husband. Whenever I feel discouraged about the "smallness" of my calling, I must remind myself how great

a privilege it is to pray. That my prayers may be far more powerful than any other ministry I may ever have or see.

3. The women in the Bible have already given me beautiful examples of godliness. They remind me to focus on generosity, teaching children, loving my husband, following Jesus, caring for those in distress, teaching younger women to love their husbands and children, remembering those in prison, comforting the orphan and widow, serving the believers, hospitality, and so much more that I can do as a woman.

Bonus Content: Earth is Not Enough

There's a song by the famous Irish band U2 with the words, "I still haven't found what I'm looking for." The song seems to get played over and over again in stores. Maybe it keeps shoppers shopping longer. They keep thinking they haven't found what they're looking for. I've heard that for every extra minute spent in a store, the buyer spends an additional $1.30.

The song also seems to stick in my head after I hear it. And the lyrics are haunting. Have you ever felt that there's something more you need in life, if only you knew what it was? I've literally walked around Sam's Club praying, "Lord, if there is something I could buy that would make my life easier, please show me what it is." In that sense, I still haven't found what I'm looking for.

But even more than a purchase, have you ever felt like something was missing from your life? Have you ever wondered if maybe there is something better out there in life that others have, but you don't know about it? When money is tight, it seems like money is the answer. When money is abundant, maybe looking prettier is the answer. If you are single, maybe getting married is the answer. If you're married, maybe having kids is the answer. If you have kids, maybe having grandkids is the answer. If you don't like your job, maybe a better job is the answer. If you like your job but you're tired of working, maybe retirement is the answer. And the list could go on and on.

Though all these things can be wonderful, we are never fully satisfied by any of them. And that's because neither singleness, nor marriage, nor a great marriage, nor money, nor beauty, nor anything else, can ever fully satisfy the greatest and deepest longings of our soul. We have a greater longing than the things of this earth can satisfy.

And this strange longing and aching and discouragement—we all have in common. Even the Psalmist King David wrote, "Why are you in despair, O my soul? And why have you become disturbed within me?" (Psalm 42:5).

Feeling sad is normal and can even be biblical. I think life itself has always had some degree of inescapable sadness—for every single person alive. We inherited this sorrow from Adam, we find some relief in Christ here on earth, and we will one day find ultimate relief when we enter eternity with Christ.

And because we will never be truly satisfied until we awake in the likeness of Christ, we know that our emptiness, that our longing for heaven, won't be satisfied until heaven. We will be dissatisfied with this life because we are created for something better.

THE SHARED ACHE

This shared sadness, this strange longing, this ache deep in our hearts is only appeased but never fully satisfied while we are on earth. And while the Bible tells us that those who do not obey God or know Him have many sorrows, even those of us who desire to please God from the very depths of our being still have a shared pain because we all share the same sin nature (Psalm 32:10).

That's why I'm so comforted that some of the Bible's greatest heavyweights have talked about this dissatisfaction with life. We learn about Jacob in Genesis, the first book in the Bible. Jacob is a huge part of Biblical history. Jacob's father was Isaac and his grandfather was Abraham. And God loved Jacob before he was born. The Bible says that when Rebekah "had conceived twins by one man, our father Isaac; for though the twins were not yet born and had not done anything good or bad, so that God's purpose according to His choice would stand, not because of works but because of Him who calls, it was said to her, 'THE OLDER WILL SERVE THE YOUNGER' Just as it is written, 'JACOB I LOVED, BUT ESAU I HATED.'" Whoa! God chose Jacob and loved him before he ever even did anything good or commendable.

Not only did Jacob have God's favor, his descendants became their own nation. While Jacob and his family were traveling, Jacob sent his family on ahead one night and made plans to catch up the next day. That night, an angel wrestled with Jacob until morning. During this theophany—a manifestation of God in the Bible that is tangible to the senses —God changed Jacob's name to Israel and promised that a nation would come from him.

Jacob also had twelve sons which became the twelve tribes of Israel. He was wealthy and had a beautiful wife named Rebekah, plus a second wife named Leah.

Jacob's life on earth was pretty good. Wealth. Check. Beautiful wife. Check. Lots of kids. Check. Chosen by God. Check. Father of an entire nation. Check. Grandson of Abraham, the father of faith. Check.

Yet with all this, Jacob still said, "The years of my sojourning are one hundred and thirty; few and unpleasant have been the years of my life, nor have they attained the years that my fathers lived during the days of their sojourning" (Genesis 47:9). Even with all Jacob had, he still felt unsatisfied.

Another famous and godly man is Moses. When the Israelites were slaves in Egypt, God appeared to Moses in a burning bush and instructed Moses to lead the Israelites out of slavery. While they were fleeing from Pharaoh and the Egyptian armies, God used Moses to part the Rea Sea so the Israelites could walk across on dry land. While Moses travelled with the Israelites, God gave him the Ten Commandments and showed Moses His glory.

But even though Moses was the leader of a nation, and even though He spoke with God, and even though He saw miracles with his own eyes, he still reflected on this life here on earth saying, "Seventy years are given to us! Some may even reach eighty. But even the best of these years are filled with pain and trouble; soon they disappear, and we are gone" (Psalm 90:10 NLT).

The next famous man I want us to think about is David. God called David "a man after my heart" (Acts 13:22). David is famous for his victory over Goliath the Philistine. The Philistines were at war with the Israelites. Goliath, a gigantic Philistine warrior, proclaimed that if someone would fight him, the loser of the fight and his country would serve the winner of the fight and his country.

Because David had already killed a lion and a bear as a shepherd, King Saul let David fight. After David's victory, he became famous throughout all Israel. And when Saul died, David became the king of Israel. He had multiple wives, many children, and a successful reign. Though David wasn't perfect, he was still a great example of godliness and the author of many of the Psalms from the book of Psalms in the Old Testament.

Yet David spoke about the same ache that Jacob and Moses shared: "For my life is spent with sorrow and my years with sighing; my strength has failed because of my iniquity, and my body has wasted away" (Psalm 31:10). David's success did not insulate him from the sorrow of this life.

Though David is the most famous author contributing to the book of Psalms, another great man, Asaph, contributed the second greatest number of the known authors, since fifty of the Psalms are written by unknown authors. He wrote twelve Psalms total, including one of my favorite Psalms and chapters in the Bible, Psalm 73. Asaph was a Levitical singer, a leader of the singers, a musician, and a seer (1 Chronicles 15:19, 16:37; 2 Chronicles 29:30). Asaph's full-time job was to minister before the ark of the Lord. In other words, Asaph was a full-time worship leader and songwriter. And this was during the time when the ark of the covenant of God was in the tent of worship. Asaph had one of the best, most visible ministries in Israel, worshiping God all day long and leading others in worship.

And yet Asaph still said, "Surely in vain I have kept my heart pure and washed my hands in innocence; For I have been stricken all day long and chastened every morning" (Psalm 73: 13-14). Asaph still wrestled with the feelings of frustration and disappointment that we wrestle with now. Even as a great and famous worship leader, he was still not fully satisfied here on earth.

We've talked about men with different yet amazing positions and lives: The man who began a nation, the man who received the law from God, the man after God's own heart and the great king of Israel, and the worship leader of Israel.

Now let's look at one of the most important prophets, a man who was a mouthpiece for God. God came to Jeremiah and said, "Before I formed you in the womb I knew you, and before you were born I consecrated you; I have appointed you a prophet to the nations" (Jeremiah 1:5). When Jeremiah heard God's words, he felt unable live up to God's calling. Then he tells us what happened next: "Then the LORD stretched out His hand and touched my mouth, and the LORD said to me, 'Behold, I have put My words in your mouth.'"

As someone who speaks at women's events, I pray that I will say exactly what God wants me say, every time. I beg God to put His words in my mouth so that God will be pleased with what I say. But God Himself told Jeremiah that He would put His words into Jeremiah's mouth. Jeremiah wouldn't be speaking at Christian women's events—but to multiple nations!

This prophet to the nations also suffered for God, including being beaten, put in prison, and thrown into a muddy cistern. Jeremiah reflected on the sorrow and hardship of life, saying, "I am the man who has seen affliction because of the rod of His wrath. He has driven me and made me walk in darkness and not in light...He has besieged and encompassed me with bitterness and hardship...My soul has been rejected from peace; I have forgotten happiness" (Lamentations 3:1-2, 5, 17). "Why did I ever come forth from the womb to look on trouble and sorrow, so that my days have been spent in shame?" (Jeremiah 20:18).

And I don't forget that Jesus was "a man of sorrows and acquainted with grief" because He bore our pain (Isaiah 53:3). There is an ache that plagues us all, a grief that is such a part of life on this sinful earth that even the godliest of men (and God Himself when He became a man) have shared this sorrow.

THE HOPE OF LIFE

This ache does not disappear when we find joy in Christ, but hope makes the ache bearable. The joy we have in Christ give us hope in life. The Bible tells us this was the case with Jesus, who "for the joy set before Him endured the cross." We endure this life and give it our best because of the joy set before us. And this anticipation of future grace gives relief from what would be otherwise an unbearable burden, a sorrow without hope.

That's why each of the men who wrote about their sorrow also went on to declare their joy, their hope, their reason for living:

Jacob: "God [...] has been my shepherd all my life to this day" (Genesis 48:15).

Moses: "O satisfy us in the morning with Your lovingkindness, that we may sing for joy and be glad all our days" (Psalm 90:14).

David: "But as for me, I trust in You, O LORD, I say, 'You are my God'…Blessed be the LORD, for He has made marvelous His lovingkindness to me in a besieged city" (Psalm 31:14, 21).

Asaph: "But as for me, the nearness of God is my good; I have made the Lord GOD my refuge, that I may tell of all Your works" (Psalm 73:28).

Jeremiah: "This I recall to my mind, therefore I have hope. The LORD'S lovingkindnesses indeed never cease, for His compassions never fail. They are new every morning; great is Your faithfulness. 'The LORD is my portion,' says my soul, 'Therefore I have hope in Him'" (Lamentations 3:21-24).

Jesus: "When he sees all that is accomplished by his anguish, he will be satisfied. And because of his experience, my righteous servant will make it possible for many to be counted righteous, for he will bear all their sins" (Isaiah 53:11).

Earth is Not Enough

"But to the Son he says, 'Your throne, O God, endures forever and ever. You rule with a scepter of justice. You love justice and hate evil. Therefore, O God, your God has anointed you, pouring out the oil of joy on you more than on anyone else" (Hebrews 1:8-9 NLT).

While every human on earth shares in the grief of sin, only those who have hope in Christ get to share the joy of awaiting eternal life. Those Scriptures give me comfort. I want you to know that you are not alone in your longing for more. We are all seeking to be fully satisfied, to be free from the sorrow and emptiness of this life.

But God has given us glimpses into His purpose for our sorrow. He has shown us in His Word how our desires to be fully satisfied are part of His complex and beautiful plan that is working even on the days when life feels dreary and plain.

And my desire is that as you trust God, you would feel comforted by the hope of heaven, that you would understand why you ache and how God will one day satisfy that ache, and that you would find joy and purpose in your life in the here as you wait for glory.

Additional resources for trusting God and growing in your relationship with Jesus are available at:

www.katiehoffman.org